Teach Your Child Spanish Through Play
A Guide and Resource for Parents

or

Spanish for Kids
Games to Help Children Learn Spanish
Language and Culture

by Starr Weems de Graffenried

Teach Your Child Spanish Through Play
A Guide and Resource for Parents
© 2008 Starr Weems de Graffenried

ISBN 978-0-9798956-0-9

1.0

Nomentira Publications
www.nomentira.com

Printed in USA

Contents

Introduction

Children are natural language learners. From babyhood they are listening to the language around them and building an implicit language system that in a few short years allows them to effectively communicate their interests and needs. Children from bilingual households listen and learn to reproduce the sounds of two languages quite effortlessly. These children naturally know which words belong to which language and seldom confuse the two. Interestingly, these children also seem to automatically know which language to speak to certain individuals and in specific situations.

There are advantages to learning a second language as a child. Many of us wait until adulthood to begin the study of a foreign language when time constraints and the distractions of daily life prevent us from ever achieving optimal proficiency. Children learn another language more quickly and easily and tend to retain the new language better than adults. Studies show that bilingual children demonstrate enhanced creativity and higher order thinking skills, show increased academic achievement and even learn to read more readily than their monolingual counterparts. In addition to these developmental advantages, the bilingual child reaps a practical skill that will later help him to effectively function in our increasingly complex multicultural society.

The child of a bilingual parent has a distinct advantage when it comes to language learning. The child is naturally surrounded by the sounds of the language and receives hours of meaningful input which builds the implicit language system without any special effort on the part of the caretaker. This is not the case when a parent is not a native speaker. However, it is not impossible for the monolingual parent to introduce a second language into the home. Introduction of a second language by a monolingual parent takes some thought and planning, but it can add an enjoyable element to family life that benefits everyone involved.

How to Use This Book

Teaching a foreign language to your child when that language is also foreign to you takes a little creativity. The activities presented in this book are designed to manufacture situations in which your child will readily absorb the new language, just as though he or she were being brought up in a bilingual environment. Children naturally learn through play and normal daily activity. Children who grow up in a bilingual household speak the language because they experienced the language in natural situations, not because their parents sat them down and made them memorize flashcards. The activities in this book should be treated as a learning time that doubles as quality playtime with your child. Activities should not feel like a lesson. Don't force your child to participate in an activity that he or she does not enjoy, but rather play with your child. Do not become impatient if your child refuses to perform by speaking Spanish at first. Remember that your child listened to and understood English long before he or she could produce it. Sometimes your child might seem to understand what you are saying, but might answer you in English. Continue to expose your child to the second language, and the child will benefit.

Part One of this book focuses on ways that you can maximize your child's language development outside of your direct instruction. The more of these suggestions that you can implement, the more progress you will see. Don't think of this as an all or nothing endeavor - consider each suggestion in the light of what seems right for you and your family.

Part Two is full of vocabulary activities which are compiled into thematic sets. You can pick and choose which activities are most relevant to your life and which match your child's interests at the time. You might notice that some of the activities can be modified to include different vocabulary or to better fit your child's age and developmental level. Most of these activities are appropriate for children ages 2-10, but can be easily modified to suit any age. Please feel free to individualize any activity for your child and to use these ideas as a springboard from which you can create your own language opportunities. If your child participates in formal language classes, you can use these activities to help your child practice and supplement language that he or she has already learned.

For each thematic set, you will find a vocabulary list. This list is for your reference when you conduct the activities with your child. Feel free to use a dictionary to add words and expressions that you feel are relevant. If you are worried about pronunciation, there are dozens of free online dictionaries and language learning sites that can provide audio support for the vocabulary. A helpful resource for caretaker vocabulary is a book and CD set by Ana Lomba and Marcela Summerville called *Play and Learn Spanish*. See the resource directory at the end of the book for more information.

Feel free to delete any word that you do not feel is important at this time. Make the program work for you. If at first you find it difficult to remember the vocabulary yourself while conducting the activities, copy the words onto an index card and keep it handy for reference. Consider completing a language learning program for adults to help you stay a few steps in front of your child linguistically. There are some suggestions for adult language programs in the resource directory.

Your attitude during the activities and reactions to your child when he or she uses the language can make or break the acquisition process. Your child is seeking your attention. If your child uses the new language, respond quickly and enthusiastically, even if this means stopping in the middle of something that you are doing. If your child learns that using Spanish is likely to get a quick response from you, this will encourage repeated use of the language. If you would like to test this theory, provide a quick response the first time your child hears and repeats a curse word. You can bet that this language will be used as long as it generates attention! Additionally, resist the urge to correct your child's Spanish pronunciation or to withhold a response until the child repeats a word correctly. It is best to simply reward a child for his or her linguistic efforts rather than to demand perfection. This will encourage continued practice and progress in the language.

Part Three provides a framework for teaching culture. You will find an explanation of how culture and language learning are related as well as activities to promote cultural understanding. The culture section does not focus on any one Spanish-speaking country, but provides activities that you can tailor to fit to your particular target country. This section includes a calendar with the holidays of the Spanish-speaking world. The culture activities are not meant to be conducted after, but along with the vocabulary activities.

Part Four discusses how to continue Spanish with your child as he or she grows. You will learn how to create your own activities to fit your child's changing needs as well as special considerations for preteen and high school learners.

Part Five will talk about language resources. You will learn how to evaluate resources and a directory will be provided to help you find books, language programs, cultural information and more. This section contains a list of the major Spanish-speaking countries as well as a Glossary of linguistic and education terms that appear throughout the text. You may want to review these terms before embarking on your language journey.

Frequently Asked Questions

What age should my child begin learning Spanish?

Introducing a foreign language can be done at any age, but early introduction of the language produces the best results. If possible, introduce the sounds of the language from birth. This will help your child to easily reproduce the sounds of the language later on. Linguists refer to the first years of life as the "critical period" for language learning. During the critical period, neural pathways related to language are being developed. Children who are exposed to a language during this period do not lose the ability to make its sounds later in life. Even if exposure to the language is halted during early childhood and the vocabulary is forgotten, the ability to produce native pronunciation is retained. Those who begin a foreign language later in life may achieve fluency, but rarely speak without accent. Children who have lifelong, continued exposure to a language beginning between birth to ages two or three normally have a native-like linguistic ability and no trace of a foreign accent. This is not to say that if you do not introduce your child to Spanish between birth and ages two or three that he or she will never speak like a native. A perfect accent is simply much more likely if the new language is begun during this time frame.

If you do not start from birth, the very early years of childhood between the ages of two and four are usually the easiest for introducing a foreign language. At this very young age, children are less likely to balk at the switch from English to Spanish. Two or three year olds are often just as happy to watch their favorite program in Spanish as they are to watch it in English. They are in the process of rapidly building vocabulary and grammar in their first language and have no problems absorbing a second language at the same time.

Children between the ages of five and ten also learn language very quickly and easily, but this age can be much more challenging for the introduction of a foreign language. This is due to the fact that children can develop strong opinions and must have motivation to progress in the language. What was not questioned at all at the age of two or three suddenly demands a purpose at the age of five or six. If the interest is not just naturally there for language learning, then you must create interest by establishing a purpose for learning. The activities must be enjoyable. You might set a purpose for learning the language through planning a trip, making friends with a native speaker or somehow making Spanish a part of something that your child is already intensely interested in.

Children older than age 10 still learn language quite easily when they are provided with entertaining learning opportunities, but waiting until adolescence is not advised. While they are perfectly capable of learning, adolescents and teenagers are often embarrassed by the production of the new sounds that is required by speaking a foreign language and become suddenly resistant to learning. They are intensely aware of their peers and terrified of making a mistake, which limits speaking practice. Ironically, this is when most school systems choose to begin their language programs. However, if your child is in this age range, please don't think that you have missed the window of opportunity. If an older child has the proper attitude towards the target language and culture, then language learning can still proceed rapidly and easily.

So, when should you begin to teach your child Spanish? As soon as possible. It is never too late, but the earlier you begin, the easier it will be for both parent and child.

What if I don't speak Spanish?

It's true- having prior knowledge of the language that you plan to teach your child is an advantage. If you already know Spanish, the process of teaching your child will take much less effort. However, there is plenty that you can do to introduce Spanish into your home while you are learning it yourself. To effectively present basic vocabulary to your child, you only need to stay a few steps ahead of him or her linguistically.

The best thing for you to do is to begin an adult language learning program immediately. Even completing a few lessons will probably give you the basic knowledge you need to begin teaching your child. You could look into attending a formal language class through a local university or private teacher or you could just complete a program on your own. The resource directory at the end of this book mentions several quality programs that you can use to begin your study. I absolutely love the Rosetta Stone program. This program is quite pricey, but worth it. If you don't have the money to spend, there are online language resources mentioned in the directory that offer free lessons. Most of the sites listed have audio support . You might find inexpensive programs at garage sales, library discard sales, secondhand shops, Ebay or on clearance at your local bookstore. The idea is simply to get started on something so that you will be at least slightly ahead of your child for each activity.

Section One in this book about ways to maximize Spanish language development applies not only to your child but also to you. Read the suggestions in Section One and decide how many of them that you can incorporate. Surround yourself with the Spanish language at every opportunity. Practice speaking every chance you get. Put yourself in contact with native speakers and don't be afraid to talk to them! Do anything you can to expose yourself to the language. If you are considering teaching Spanish to your child, then you already have the most important component for learning: motivation. With a little effort, your personal language learning should take off and teaching your child will become much easier.

At the very least, you should try to learn the vocabulary associated with each activity prior to introducing it to your child. Find audio support for each word in one of the online dictionaries mentioned in the resource directory or ask for help from a native speaker. Practice saying each word before introducing it to your child.

Make up mnemonic devices to help yourself remember the vocabulary. For example, if you are trying to remember the word *cama* (bed), think of a creative way to remember that word. *Cama* sounds a little similar to the English word "coma." Tell yourself, "It's like I'm in a <u>coma</u> when I'm asleep in my <u>cama</u>." Or you could picture an overenthusiastic English teacher who wears pajamas covered in semicolons, sleeps on an exclamation point- shaped pillow and in a bed shaped like a <u>comma</u>.

You can also make the mnemonic devices more elaborate in the form of wacky stories. For example, let's say that you are trying to remember that *rojo* means "red." *Rojo* is pronounced "row-hoe." Let's say that there are two rowboats having a race- a green boat and a red boat. The man in the green boat was also a gardener, so he had plenty of garden utensils lying around. He got a bright idea to replace the red boat's oars with a garden hoe, but the man in the red boat didn't notice because the ends of the sticks were down in the water. When the race began, the green boat sped off, but the red boat couldn't seem to get going. He pulled an oar out of the water only to discover that it had been replaced with a garden hoe. The man in the red boat yells, "Hey! I can't <u>ROW</u> with a <u>HOE</u>!" This way, you can remember that red is *rojo* or "ROW HOE."

The sillier and more disgusting your mnemonic devices, the more memorable they will be. It might seem difficult at first to come up with creative ways to remember words, but with time you will develop the skill of creating mnemonic devices automatically when you come in contact with a new word. In the meantime, make yourself a little cheat sheet just in case you forget words in the middle of the lesson. You do not have to be an expert or wait until you have mastered the language to teach your child basic vocabulary, you just need to be resourceful.

In addition to learning all that you can on your own, you will be supplementing your teaching with the use of materials such as music, books, contact with native speakers, movies and television where appropriate. This will benefit your child by exposing him to native accents and new vocabulary and will provide a strong base for future language development. Your child will benefit from even the most casual exposure to the new language.

Should I supplement my instruction with formal language lessons?

This depends on your child. For some children, taking formal lessons can make language learning suddenly seem like work instead of a fun game and can actually hinder instead of help the acquisition process. This is especially true when the child's Spanish teacher focuses heavily on grammar and meaningless language drills. Having your child take lessons can expose the hidden educational agenda of your language activities and destroy the magic, making some children suddenly hesitant to participate in what used to just be fun playtime with mom or dad. For other children, formal language lessons are just what they need to make their language learning take off. If they have a very inspiring teacher who makes learning fun, then formal lessons can encourage your child to spend even more time practicing the language on his or her own.

So how do you know whether formal lessons will help or hinder your child? Think about how your child reacts to a structured learning environment. If your child goes to preschool or day care, ask your child's teacher if he or she is resistant or open during structured educational activities such as learning the alphabet, numbers and shapes. When your child talks about day care or preschool, does he or she seem excited about the lessons? Has your child taken any other types of lessons in the past such as ballet, piano or art? How did he or she respond? If you already know that your child responds well to structured educational situations, then it might be worth it to give formal Spanish lessons a shot. However, if your child responds with distaste to structured lessons, you would do well to just complete activities with him or her on your own, treating the activities as games that have nothing at all to do with school.

You must also ask yourself whether your child has the time and energy for Spanish lessons. The Spanish activities that you will be conducting with him are fun games that fit right in to your normal daily life. Formal lessons will involve cutting in to your child's free time, which can often seem like a chore if your child is already in school or involved in other organized activities. It is best to begin lessons during a time that your child is not overwhelmed.

If you have determined that your child would benefit from formal Spanish lessons, it is imperative that you find the right teacher for your child. A bad experience with an instructor can taint your child's attitudes towards language learning forever. A good language teacher will help stimulate interest in the language, create engaging and enjoyable lessons, be sensitive to the unique needs of your child and will help to cultivate a positive attitude towards the target language and culture.

It is always nice if you can find a native speaker to teach your child, but sometimes the best language teachers are ones who have had to learn the language themselves. You should be more concerned with the quality of actual instruction than whether or not the teacher is a native speaker. When you interview teachers, be sure to arrange a trial lesson that you can be present for so that you can observe student- teacher dynamics. Does your child seem to respond well to the techniques? Is the teacher patient? Is vocabulary presented in context or in isolated lists for memorization? Do the lessons seem fun or is your child likely to burn out quickly? While watching the lesson, do you learn the vocabulary yourself?

It can sometimes be difficult to find quality language teachers for private instruction. One good way to find a teacher is to get in contact with the Spanish teachers at local schools. Often, school teachers offer private lessons on the side or know someone who does. You can also run an ad in the local paper or do an Internet search for teachers in your area. Some cities even have language centers where youngsters can take Spanish lessons as part of a class.

I've heard that there are lots of different types of Spanish. If I teach my child one type, will he be understood by all Spanish speakers?

The Spanish language does vary from location to location. When Spanish traveled from Spain to the Americas, factors such as isolation from the mother country, influence of indigenous languages and the slang commonly spoken among sailors made their marks on the language.

There are also regional differences in the Spanish spoken within Spain itself. Standard Spanish, or *Castellano*, carries a slight lisp. The Spanish spoken in Andalucía in the south of Spain has a very distinct accent characterized by the absence of this lisp and the slurring of certain word endings such as *-ado*. During the Spanish population of the Americas, Spaniards who came to the New World left from Andalucían ports, and they sometimes had to spend months in Andalucía before setting out to sea. The majority of sailors on the ships sailing toward the Americas were also Andalucían. This means that any Spaniard going to the New World by ship had to be in contact with the Andalucían dialect (in very close quarters) for at least 40 days while at sea. Meanwhile, during those 40 or more days, the slang spoken among the sailors began to leak into the language. This language was then deposited onto the shores of the New World, already different from the standard Castellano.

Once this modified Andalucían dialect reached the Americas,

it was destined to be further altered by the indigenous languages. The New World had objects, animals, people and plant life that the Spanish of the time had no words to describe. Sometimes the indigenous word was adopted into the language (like *chocolate*) and sometimes a new word that sounded much like the indigenous word was added . The language continued to evolve, separated from the mother country.

In the meantime, the Spanish spoken in Spain also began to evolve. Before the sixteenth century, the pronoun *vos* was used in Spain to refer to nobility and *tú* to refer to those who were familiar. Once a new title of honor (*vuestra merced* or *usted*) came into fashion, *vos* was dropped from formal use. It just so happened that during the transition from *vos* to *usted* in Spain, the Spanish conquest of the Americas was taking place. Some Spaniards populating the New World used *vos* and some didn't. The result was that in parts of Central and South America *vos* was preserved while its use dropped completely out of the Spanish spoken in Spain.

So here were people with a southern Spanish accent continuing to use words and grammatical constructions that had already gone out of fashion in the mother country. They were mixing that language with sailor slang and adding in some Native American words. These people were almost completely out of contact with the people in the mother country. Meanwhile, the dialect in the mother country was evolving as well. Time passed and certain words and expressions fell into and out of favor with the people. Each generation had its own vernacular. The dialects grew farther and farther apart.

Additionally, the Spanish language changed from region to region within the Americas. After all, there were many different Native American languages to influence the Spanish depending on where each group of Spaniards settled. Those groups of people were also isolated from one another and each of their dialects evolved independently of one another.

Fast forward a few hundred years. It's really a wonder that Spanish speaking people across the globe can understand one another at all, but they can! Sure, there are lots of differences in the Spanish spoken from country to country and even in the Spanish spoken from region to region within each country, but try to think of those differences in terms of the differences that occur in the English language.

We have many different varieties of English in the United States that have their own accents, words and expressions. Northerners have different accents from Southerners. East coast residents have a different accent from those on the West coast. If you are familiar with the dialects, you can almost always identify what state someone is from when he or she opens his mouth to speak. Even within states, there is almost always a difference in the accents of people who live in the city versus those who live in rural areas. There are even accents specific to certain age and ethnic groups. But it isn't just accents- we actually have different words and expressions to describe things as well. Outside of the South, not many people know that "fixin' to" means "about to" or that if you say that someone is "ill" that they are not sick but rather in a bad mood. Depending on where you live in this country, a can of cola can be a "soda," a "coke," a "pop" or just a "cold drink". And that's just in the United States.

If we look outside of the United States, we have even more dialectical differences in the English language. Just within the United Kingdom, a tiny area compared to the United States, we have hundreds of different dialects. In British English, for example, trousers are pants and pants are underwear. A courgette is a zucchini and a biscuit is a cookie. Fries are chips and if the milk has "gone off," then it is spoiled. And what about the English spoken in Canada, Australia, New Zealand, Jamaica, South Africa, Belize, the Virgin Islands and many other locations throughout the world? They all have language variations particular to their areas and sub variations depending on age, education level and social class.

But can we all understand one another? Well, yes, for the most part. There can be minor misunderstandings here and there and sometimes we have to ask one another to repeat something, but it's still English and we can make sense of it. To make things easier, we have a sort of standard English that is used for things like television programs. Spanish is the same way. There are certainly marked differences in the Spanish used in the different regions of the world, but Spanish speakers worldwide do understand one another. There exists a sort of standard Spanish that everyone can easily understand. This standard Spanish is what is normally presented in classrooms and language programs.

If you are planning a trip to or have a close friend from a certain country, then you might try to learn some of the vocabulary specific to that location. Otherwise, don't worry too much about the type of Spanish that your child is learning.

What are the benefits to teaching my child Spanish?

One obvious benefit to taking the time to teach your child Spanish is the opportunity to spend more quality time playing with and enjoying your child. It is very fulfilling to watch your child progress at something that you are teaching and it feels good to know that you are providing your children with an opportunity to learn something that will continue to open doors for them rest of their lives. Knowing Spanish will increase opportunities for your child socially, intellectually and financially.

Learning a second language and culture prepares your child for success in our increasingly global society. Being proficient in a second language increases marketability in the business world and makes your child a more effective global citizen. There are neurological benefits to learning a second language during childhood as well. A large percentage of neural pathways are formed before the age of eight. Mastering a foreign language early in life triggers brain growth. Early second language learning is associated with academic success and increased problem solving and communication skills as an adult.

Teaching your child Spanish early on also sets the stage for easily learning a third language. The more languages that your child speaks, the easier it is to learn even more. If it turns out that Spanish does not happen to be the language he needs to know later in life, it will be no trouble for him to subsequently add a third language to his repertoire.

Won't learning another language confuse my child? Will he get them mixed up?

No. Children automatically categorize language. Sometimes you might hear a child mix two languages, but this is temporary and usually only occurs when the child does not have the words to say something in one language or the other. Children seem to understand which words belong to which languages and even seem to know who to speak certain languages to without being taught.

The vocabulary activities in this book don't involve much reading and writing at first. Why not?

The beginning vocabulary activities do not involve reading and writing for several reasons. Firstly, I wanted to make the activities accessible to a wide range of ages. So many children's language programs rely on the child's ability to read in order to present the new language. I wanted these activities to be for toddlers and preschoolers as well as for school aged children.

Another reason is the fun factor. Some children equate reading and writing with a school-type situation and I wanted these activities to be fun games that mimic natural interaction with your child. These activities should not have an "educational" flavor to them until interest in the second language is firmly established.

It is also beneficial for your child to have a strong base in the spoken language before he or she begins reading. Often times, children who have already learned to read in their own language will suddenly begin mispronouncing words once they start applying English pronunciation rules to printed Spanish words. For instance, the Spanish word for "hello" is *hola*, pronounced "oh-la." The "h" is silent. Students tend to pronounce this word perfectly until they see it written down. Once they see the "h", they can't seem to get it out of their heads. Suddenly "oh-la" becomes "hoe-la" no matter how many times they are corrected. This does not happen when there has been sufficient practice with the spoken language before the written language is introduced.

There are some activities with reading and writing that appear in the later activities and in the culture section. It will be up to you to decide whether or not your child is ready for reading and writing in Spanish. Nobody knows your child better than you. You should pick and choose which activities are right for your child.

How much time should I spend on Spanish activities with my child?

Try not to think of teaching Spanish to your child in terms of blocks of time where instruction lasts for one hour and then the rest of your day goes on as normal. Think of Spanish as something that you are incorporating into daily life at every opportunity. If you know the Spanish word for something, use it instead of the English whenever possible.

Part I
Ways to Maximize Spanish Language Development

Make Language Learning a Family Affair

Make learning Spanish a family project. You will have to work on your Spanish in order to stay ahead of your child, so why not have all of the adults and older children take a Spanish class together or complete a home Spanish program together? The more people in your family who are practicing the new language, the more Spanish your child will absorb. This is also an opportunity for your family to spend some quality time doing something enjoyable. Increase the motivation by setting a group goal such as learning enough Spanish to take a vacation to a Spanish-speaking country.

Many colleges and community centers offer Spanish classes through continuing education programs. Sometimes a formal class is easier to stick with than completing a program at home. Often, time constraints and daily responsibilities can keep you from spending as much time with a home language program as you would like. Carving out a specific time slot for a formal class can be a great way to keep you on track. If you do decide to complete a program on your own, be sure to block out a time slot for it that everyone can be present for. Make it a priority. It will probably be useful to set rewards for yourselves to keep the excitement alive and to avoid burnout. For instance, once you have completed a certain number of lessons, plan a fun night out to practice your Spanish at a local restaurant, go to see a Spanish movie or schedule a group salsa lesson. Set long-term goals for your language development and also short-term goals along the way. Revisit old lessons from time to time so that you can see how far you have come with your language learning. There is a list of language programs and how to obtain them in the resource directory.

Consider designating a specific time slot or activity as a "Spanish only zone" to encourage language practice. The Spanish only zone could be a shared mealtime, room in the house or entire day of the week. You can make a game out of it by having anyone who slips up and uses English in the Spanish only zone be responsible for the dishes or another chore. In addition to improving your own language ability, this practice will provide even more quality input for your child. The more that Spanish is spoken around your child, especially in everyday family situations, the more language will be absorbed. This is how he or she learned English.

Consider Bilingual Childcare

If your child attends a daycare or preschool, look into programs that offer bilingual education. Two-way Spanish bilingual education programs are becoming more and more popular as the demand for Spanish grows. These programs combine native Spanish speakers and native English speakers for instruction in both languages. In addition to the obvious benefit of having direct instruction in the foreign language, there is the opportunity for cultural interchange among the students. Students of Spanish are exposed to native accents and are in a good position to make friends with native speakers, which will aid language acquisition.

If cost or availability precludes you from enrolling your child in a center where Spanish is actively taught, consider sending your child somewhere that has a high concentration of Spanish speaking children. Your child is bound to be exposed to Spanish and is likely to make friends with children with whom he or she can converse.

If someone takes care of your child in your home, consider hiring someone who is bilingual. You might find this person through word of mouth, a local agency or an ad in the paper. Ask this person to use only the target language while in your home. Even children who balk at their parents' use of a foreign language are usually accepting of someone outside of the family speaking it, especially if they think that this person might have trouble conversing in English. Ask the caretaker to read to your child in Spanish, play games with him or her and perhaps to talk about his or her native country and culture. Ask the sitter to talk more than he or she normally would to maximize exposure to the language. For instance, tell her to talk about everything that she does. If he or she is making a sandwich for your child, he or she should say, "I'm taking the bread out of the bag. There is cheese in the refrigerator. I am going to take it out of the refrigerator," etc. You might also talk to the caretaker about preparing authentic dishes from his or her home country. In all likelihood, he or she will be happy to share with your child about his or her native culture. It is nice to know that while you have to be away from your child that a competent person is taking care of things and at the same time providing a valuable learning experience.

For some people, live-in help is a wonderful option. It can be surprisingly inexpensive through an excellent, government regulated program called Au Pair. The U.S. Department of State grants educated young foreign individuals between the ages of 18-26 with no criminal record and professional childcare experience permission through the Au Pair program to come to the United States and provide in-home childcare for interested families. For families with children under two years of age, the Au Pair is required to have 200 hours of practical child care experience. Au Pair programs generally last for one summer to one year, but can be granted a one-year extension. Au Pairs provide up to 45 hours of child care per week while completing a six hour educational requirement at a nearby University. According to the Au Pair program, the Au Pair must be provided with meals, a private bedroom, 1 1/2 days off per week plus one full weekend off per month, an amount toward the costs of coursework, two weeks paid vacation per year and a weekly amount tied to the minimum wage. In 2008, the minimum payment will be $176.85, in 2009 it will be $195.75. Regulations say that Au Pairs should not work more than 10 hours per day toward their 45 weekly hours. Up to date information about this program can be found on the U.S. Department of State website listed in the resource directory.

There is another Au Pair program for school aged children called US EduCare Au Pair. The Au Pair participating in this program works fewer hours than the full-time Au Pair for a lower price (currently $105 per week). The family is still responsible for a portion of education costs for the Au Pair, who must complete 12 hours of coursework.

Hosting an Au Pair can provide an invaluable experience for the entire family. It is a rare opportunity for almost full-time exposure to the language and culture of another country while remaining at home. When you compare the costs to normal, in-home childcare costs, you will find these prices very inexpensive. The resource directory lists contact information for several Au Pair agencies.

If you are a stay at home parent who does not need day time childcare, consider using a native speaker as a babysitter for regular evenings out. Ask him or her to speak Spanish to your children and to read Spanish books to them while in your home. A good way to find a Spanish speaking babysitter might be to ask for a recommendation from a local high school teacher. High school teachers are normally in contact with hundreds if not thousands of teenagers and normally have a very good idea about which ones would be reliable.

The effects of bilingual childcare can be comparable to those of growing up in a home with a native speaker parent. It is well worth the effort to research your childcare options to see if a bilingual environment can be provided during the times when you have to be away.

Exchange Students

Hosting an exchange student is another way to bring culture into your home. The situation with an exchange student is a little different than that of an Au Pair, as an exchange student is normally there to learn English. However, an exchange student living in your home will be a valuable source of cultural information and an easy reference if you happen to have a question about the language.

Typically, to host an exchange student, all you have to have is an extra bed, a way to get the student to and from school and an open, friendly home. Exchange students tend to quickly become like family members and often establish lifelong relationships with the host family. You might even eventually visit your student in his or her own country later on.

There are many exchange programs out there and some of them are listed in the resource directory. To become a host family, contact an agency. Typically, they will send you the profiles of students from different countries and you will choose a student of the age and gender which interests you. You will choose whether to host a student for a semester or an entire academic year. There are some programs that also offer summer or one month exchanges. You will normally be put in contact with a local coordinator who can help you deal with any problems that might arise during your exchange student's stay in the country.

Pen Pals

A pen pal relationship is a wonderful way to help your child learn about another culture. Pen pals can be found through a pen pal agency, through exchange students or other native speakers with whom you come in contact. The best thing is to try to establish a family pen pal relationship with a foreign family. There is a detailed section about how to make the most of a pen-pal relationship in Part Three of this book. There is a list of pen pal agencies in the resource directory. Make sure that you keep the pen pal relationship interesting for a pre-reader by exchanging pictures and perhaps music, cartoon clippings and food items.

Create a Network of Spanish Speakers

Find or create a group of Spanish speakers with whom to practice. Sometimes, there might be an existing Spanish conversation group in your area that you and your family could join. Ask around to see if such a group already exists. Spanish teachers and professors at local schools and universities are likely to know if your area has any group like this. If no group like this exists, start one of your own! You could place an ad in the local paper, put the word out in the community through Spanish teachers, make fliers to place around town or go through an online community. There are websites such as Meetup.com which allow people to connect and meet with local individuals with similar interests. There are a list of many of these websites in the resource directory.

Growing Your Bilingual Community

If you choose to start your own group, the quickest way to grow your bilingual community is to combine all of the above ideas. Create a group on every website that you can find and link them all together. For instance, let's say that you create a group on Meetup. com and you decide to make that your main group. Meetup is a nice site to manage a group because it has a convenient calendar of events that sends out automatic reminders as well as having an RSVP function and message boards for discussion. The site also gives you ideas to help you increase the size of your group. In addition to your Meetup group, you should also create a group through Tribe, Yahoo, Google, etc. and direct all members of those groups toward your Meetup group. Meanwhile, you should also distribute fliers, put the word out through people that you know and run an ad. Most communities have a small Spanish newspaper. See about placing an ad in that paper as well. If you do not want people to call you, your ads and fliers can direct people toward your online group, which will allow you to communicate by email and message boards.

A language group can serve several functions, but it must be maintained and must provide a variety of activities to cater to all of the group's members to help keep the interest alive. Within your group, you might set up a bilingual playgroup, family social gatherings, resource swaps, intercambio programs, adult conversation groups, language tutoring, game groups, holiday parties and dinner meetings at local restaurants.

Bilingual Playgroups

For your needs, creating a bilingual playgroup within your Spanish community is one of the most beneficial things that you can do for your child's language development. Children learn language from other children. My four year old nephew learned Ukrainian in one summer just by living next door to and playing with a visiting child who spoke only Ukrainian. The desire to play with and understand one another is a powerful force which encourages communication. A great way to encourage your child's friendship with Spanish speakers is to join a bilingual playgroup. A bilingual playgroup is ideal because you will have the opportunity to practice your Spanish with other bilingual parents while your children play together.

You might start by meeting once a week or so at a local park or public swimming pool. Later, as your group grows more closely knit, you might take turns hosting the group at one another's homes. Other fun activities for playgroups are zoo outings, picnics or a short hike at a local nature trail. Every new experience is an opportunity for your child to use new and different vocabulary to converse about his surroundings.

Intercambio Programs

Intercambio programs are an excellent way to increase your vocabulary and get many of your language questions answered by a native speaker. An intercambio program is where a native English speaker who wants to improve Spanish speaking skills and a native Spanish speaker who wants to improve English speaking skills get together and help one another. These programs are a great way to get native speakers to participate in your group. You can conduct intercambio sessions as a group or you can match up members for one on one practice.

Game Groups

Within your bilingual community, there may be individuals who are interested in getting together on a regular basis to play a card game or a particular sport. This can be a way to create a sense of community within your group and provide opportunity for language practice. Game groups can be conducted in conjunction with a children's playgroup. The children can play with one another while the adults take part in their own activity.

Exercise Groups

There are often individuals within a community who are interested in both improving language skills and physical fitness. A walking or jogging group provides an opportunity for multitasking exercise and Spanish conversation. Stay at home parents might begin a stroller group.

Movie Nights

Have a group member host a movie night to watch a family-friendly movie in Spanish. After the movie, be sure to discuss it in Spanish! This is a good activity to stimulate conversation and to provide a low-pressure environment for the first meetings.

Children's Book Club

Create a mini book club within your group for children and parents. Take turns bringing in books to read aloud to the group of children. Have discussion about the books after each reading. The children in the group can even work collaboratively to create their own book in Spanish. Have it bound and distribute it to the rest of the group. Older children can work on a newsletter for the community. These activities will promote literacy in Spanish and the children will feel proud of their accomplishments.

Dinner Night

Dinner night is one of the easiest get-togethers to plan for a conversation group. Plan to meet at a family-friendly restaurant to share a meal and Spanish conversation together. Come prepared with a few questions and conversation topics just in case the first meetings are awkward.

Holiday Parties

You can use the holiday calendar in Part Three of this book to plan parties for the holidays of the Spanish-speaking world. There is certainly no shortage of holidays to choose from. Have each person bring a dish from the country of focus, put up some decorations and have fun with the whole family. Of course you will vary your activities depending on the holiday. Use some of the activities listed in the holiday calendar for ideas.

Resource Swap

Most parents who are teaching their children a foreign language are on the constant lookout for useful materials and resources to help them. Arrange a resource swap night. Bring all of your old Spanish books, movies, magazines, music, games and toys to swap for new ones.

Television, Movies and Cartoons

Children are like little tape recorders. If your child has a favorite movie or cartoon, he or she can likely quote it from start to finish. A good way to expose your child to some quality comprehensible input to help internalize the language is to find those favorites in Spanish.

This is usually quite simple now that the audio for most DVDs includes an option for Spanish in the setup portion of the disk. With any luck, your child will enjoy watching his or her favorite show in Spanish just as much as in English and pick up some valuable language along the way. This is especially effective for very young children around 2 or 3 years of age because they seem to be less resistant to the switch from English to Spanish audio. Be sure, however, to follow the American Academy of Pediatrics recommendations on the amount of screen time your toddler should have per day.

Many Spanish channels are now available through cable or satellite television companies. If these channels carry programming that you and your family enjoy, consider adding them. Exposure to the native accents and intonation on the programs will help to improve your child's ear for the language.

Try to find some culturally authentic movies or cartoons for your child to enjoy. Culturally authentic simply means that the material is targeted towards native speakers of the language, not towards students of the language. The value of culturally authentic materials is explained further in the culture section.

Spanish Music

Music is a powerful tool that can help a child to become accustomed to the sounds of the new language and foster phonemic awareness. There are a variety of children's CDs which can be acquired through music stores, book stores and the Internet which feature culturally authentic music. Some will provide English translations to the lyrics so that you can understand what each song is about. Children can listen to the Spanish music while playing or in the car and will be singing along in Spanish in no time.

Books

There are quite a few catalogs and Internet sites where culturally authentic books can be purchased in Spanish. There are also childhood classics now being published in Spanish translation and in bilingual format with both English and Spanish. Reading to your child in Spanish will help build vocabulary and increase phonemic awareness. When reading to your child in Spanish, make your voice as expressive as possible. Make funny voices to go along with each character and create excitement with your tone. Children enjoy hearing the same book over and over, which provides repetition to further increase vocabulary. If your child can already read, Spanish picture books and coloring books are a wonderful language-building tool that your child can use on his or her own.

The key is to promoting reading in the target language is to find books that the child is interested in. Reading the instruction manual for your new electric razor to your 5 year old girl just because it is in Spanish is not going to be nearly as effective as reading her a book about a friendly unicorn. If you are fortunate enough to live in an area with a dense Spanish-speaking population, you might find that public libraries offer a good selection of Spanish children's books and might even offer a story hour in Spanish. There is a list of places to obtain children's books in Spanish in the resource directory.

Language Camps

Language immersion camps can be a way to quickly accelerate language acquisition. There are language camps for children, teenagers, adults and entire families. Some language immersion camps offer day only programs and some programs include room and board. Language camps can range from intensive weekend programs to months-long camps. Typically, there are a variety of activities conducted in the camps that are meant to encourage conversation and the use of English is strictly forbidden. Language camps normally also include a cultural component so that acquisition of language and culture happen simultaneously. There are hundreds of language camps that offer different programs and activities. A few of these programs are listed in the resource directory.

Exchanges

While bringing an exchange student into your home can be a valuable experience for the whole family, nothing compares to the benefit of being part of an exchange and absorbing language and culture while living with a host family. This type of arrangement goes far beyond experiencing the foreign culture as a tourist and lets you see how things work from the inside out. For older children and teenagers, the same exchange agencies that help you to find a foreign student to host can help with placing your child in a program.

With younger children the best type of exchange is one that parent and child can do together. This will help both you and your child's Spanish language and culture acquisition while reducing the anxiety over sending your child abroad that can occur in a traditional exchange. You will have little to lose if for whatever reason the exchange does not work out. You will simply take yourselves to a local hotel and continue your trip. Private exchanges of this nature can be arranged through mutual friends, pen pal families or an Internet service. Place yourself in contact with a family abroad who has a young child (or children) who are learning English and reach an arrangement with the family regarding the exchange.

Perhaps the parent and child will visit your country first. You will have already agreed on the amount of time you will spend in one another's homes. While your exchange family is visiting, try to gain permission from your child's teacher to allow the foreign child to come and visit the school or preschool with your child. You might also gain permission from your employer to allow the parent to come to work with you for a few days. Do your exchange family the courtesy of speaking only English while they visit you and ask them to reciprocate when you visit them.

When you go to visit your exchange family, commit to only speaking Spanish- even with your child. Before you go, learn as much as you can about the area and make a list of places that you would like to explore. Bring along a dictionary or phrase book for those times when you can not make yourself be understood. An electronic dictionary takes up much less room in your luggage and allows you to have the information right at your fingertips at all times.

Travel

The next best thing to an exchange program is foreign travel with your family. If possible, take a family vacation to a Spanish speaking location and commit to speaking Spanish as much as possible while you are there. Often, plane tickets and packages through online travel sites can be surprisingly inexpensive. Be sure to research entry requirements for the country you plan to visit and make sure your passports or other paperwork are up to date. Write the embassy for more information and look online at our government's website for travel warnings. There are some travel resources listed in the directory to get you started.

Make the most of your time abroad. Before leaving, learn as much as possible about your destination. Have your child help you plan the itinerary. There are many quality travel guides out there. My favorite brand is *Let's Go*. Make a list of sites that you would like to see while you are there. Study the food and decide what items you would like to try. Research any local festivals that might be going on while you are there. Learn a little about any historical landmarks that you plan to tour and look at pictures of them before going abroad to create interest for your child and maximize the educational experience.

Use this trip as an opportunity to teach your child new vocabulary that you are likely to have to use while you are there. Role play restaurant, hotel, telephone, taxi, train, museum and direction asking scenes with your child. Additionally, make sure your child has the vocabulary to ask for help if he or she needs it and is taught how to contact the police or embassy in the target country if an emergency situation arises.

While in the target country, use the language as much as possible. Ask for directions even if you already know where you are going, chat with locals in cafés and restaurants. Ask for food recommendations from waiters, stop people on the street and ask them where the best restaurants, movie theaters, shopping areas and parks are. In most places, people who are used to dealing with tourists speak several languages, English included. Don't let them speak English to you! Thank them for trying to make things easier for you, but explain that you are here to practice your Spanish and most people will be thrilled to help.

Surround Yourself With Spanish

If a trip to a Spanish-speaking location is not a possibility for your family, seek out the same type experience on a smaller scale: restaurant or supermarket that caters to some segment of the Spanish speaking population. With over 30 million Spanish speakers in the United States, odds are that you will have no problem finding an authentic restaurant or market. Maybe a trip to the local Mexican restaurant whereby you will commit to practicing your Spanish for the duration of the meal can become a weekly family outing. Do some shopping at a Mexican supermarket and speak to the staff in Spanish. Read all of the signs and try to acquire new vocabulary to use with your child. Surround yourself with Spanish in every possible situation and watch your Spanish language ability grow.

Part II
Vocabulary Activities

Numbers 1 - 100

1 - 20

1 uno

2 dos

3 tres

4 cuatro

5 cinco

6 seis

7 siete

8 ocho

9 nueve

10 diez

11 once

12 doce

13 trece

14 catorce

15 quince

16 dieciséis

17 diecisiete

18 dieciocho

19 diecinueve

20 veinte

30 - 100

30 treinta

40 cuarenta

50 cincuenta

60 sesenta

70 setenta

80 ochenta

90 noventa

100 cien, ciento

Numbers 20-90 follow this pattern:

21 veinte y uno

32 treinta y dos

43 cuarenta y tres

54 cincuenta y cuatro

65 sesenta y cinco

76 setenta y seis

87 ochenta y siete

98 noventa y ocho

Note: the "y" is pronounced "eee"

Number Activities

Number Stories

Many traditional children's stories and fairy tales are full of numbers. One way to introduce Spanish numbers is through story time embedding. When your child asks for a bedtime story, tell him or her a story, substituting the Spanish numbers for the English numbers. Even better is to create your own story or to modify the traditional stories to include even more numbers and repetition. My two year old daughter likes a story that we call "Sadie, Sadie the Stinky Lady" that features a woman who has gone far too long without a bath. This story changes every time we tell it, but always includes lots of numbers as Sadie counts how many bars of soap it takes to wash herself (twenty), how many teeth she uncovers when she finally brushes them (twenty again) and how many critters she washes out of her hair (usually ten). This trick is how my daughter learned her numbers in both Spanish and English. Now she can count right along with the stinky lady.

Everyday Counting

Count aloud in Spanish as often as possible in front of your child. Count steps as you climb, count apples as you put them in a bag, count how many blocks you pick up from the floor as you clean, say the numbers aloud as you dial a telephone number, etc. This is quality, meaningful input that will help your child to quickly internalize the number words.

Hide and Seek

Hide and Seek is one way to incorporate number vocabulary. You can begin by hiding your eyes and loudly counting to twenty (or one hundred) in Spanish while your child hides. As you look for your child, loudly repeat, "*¿Dónde está* _____?" (Where is <u>child's name</u>?). When you find your child, you can say, "*Te veo*" (I see you). This is a natural way for your child to learn some very valuable vocabulary during playtime.

Dough Numbers

Using modeling clay or dough, say the name of a number in Spanish and have the child make the number with the dough. If your child can not yet recognize numbers, this is a good way to introduce them. Dough numbers are great for kinesthetic learners and are just plain fun. If you feel very ambitious, you can try making the numbers out of biscuit or cookie dough to see how they bake up! This provides new opportunities for vocabulary usage when your child chooses which number he or she wants to eat.

Rayuela

Rayuela is a useful game for all sorts of vocabulary. *Rayuela* is what we usually call "hopscotch." With chalk, draw a hopscotch on the sidewalk and put numbers in each box. For children who can not recognize written numbers but who can count, fill the boxes with drawings of circles, hearts or other shapes of varying numbers. As the child lands on each box, have him or her call out the number in Spanish. A fun variation on this game is simply to draw a grid with numbers 1-100 and call out a number. The child will try to jump from one number to the other as you say it aloud.

Jump Rope and Hula Hoop

These classic outdoor activities are perfect for practicing numbers. Have a contest to see who can skip the rope the greatest number of times or who can keep the hoop going for a greater number of seconds. Count aloud, of course, in Spanish.

Bingo

Draw a grid five spaces across and five spaces down with a *libre* (free space) in the middle. Fill the spaces with numbers. As you call out the number in Spanish, you child marks it off. When he fills all five spaces either diagonally, across or down he gets a bingo. Bingo is another game that can be modified to use all sorts of vocabulary.

Colors

black = negro

blue = azul

brown = marrón, café

green = verde

grey = gris

orange = anaranjado, naranja

pink = rosado, rosa

purple = morado

red = rojo

violet = violeta

white = blanco

yellow = amarillo

Grammar note:

In Spanish, every noun has a gender. For instance, the word *silla* (chair) is feminine and *libro* (book) is masculine. This might seem strange to English speakers. The most basic rule is this: if something ends in an "o", then it is masculine. If it ends in an "a", it is feminine. There is really more to it than just that, but this is all you really need to know right now.

In Spanish, adjectives must agree in gender and number with the nouns they modify and normally follow the noun instead of preceding it as in English. Color words are adjectives. This means that they have to change to fit the nouns that you are putting them with. But here is a trick: you only have to worry about changing the ones that end in an "o" or "a". So for example:

una silla roja a red chair

unas sillas rojas some red chairs

un libro rojo a red book

unos libros rojos some red books

If this goes over your head, don't worry about it for now. Just do the best you can at introducing the color words. As your Spanish improves, you will gain an understanding of this concept.

Color Activities

Everyday Incorporation

Talk about colors at every opportunity. Name the colors of your child's toys, the produce at the supermarket, pictures in books, flowers, cars, etc. You can also ask your child, "*¿Qué color tiene?*" (What color is it?) and see if he or she can answer you. This is the simplest and most basic way to help your child learn color words in Spanish.

Coloring Book

Sit down with your child while he or she colors in a coloring book. Talk with your child about each color used. Make suggestions on which color certain items should be. Be sure that if you see anything else in the pictures that you know how to talk about in Spanish that you do so. If possible, use a Spanish coloring book and read the text to your child as he or she colors. Pick up a crayon and ask your child, "*¿Qué color tiene ?*" (What color is it?). Sometimes you can even find crayons with the Spanish color word on the side, which can be a good learning tool.

I Spy

This is a nice game to pass the time on a car ride or in a waiting room. Choose an item that you can see and tell your child what color it is. You might say, "I see something red" (*Veo algo rojo*). Your child will guess objects (in Spanish if he or she can!) until the correct item has been identified.

Magic Cookies

Separate a large batch of white icing into four bowls. Add food coloring to make one bowl yellow, one red, one blue and one white. Talk about each color with your child in Spanish. Now, experiment with mixing the colors together. What color icing do you get when you mix blue with yellow? Red with white? Mention the name for each color in Spanish as often as possible. Have your child tell you what color cookie he or she wants in Spanish. Spread the icing on a graham cracker to make a "magic cookie". Yum!

Cars

This is another travel game that incorporates colors and numbers. Each person in the car is designated a color. For instance, Mom might be *azul* and Dad might be *blanco*. Each time Mom sees a blue car on the road, she will count it. When she sees the first blue car, she will say, "*azul- uno*" and at the second blue car "*azul- dos*" and so on. Dad will do the same with white cars. The first person to spy twenty cars with their color wins.

Color Scavenger Hunt

A color scavenger hunt is fun to play outdoors, but can also be played indoors. Give your child a color in Spanish and then give him or her about 5 minutes to return with as many items with that color as possible. This is most fun as a competition between two people.

Color Memory Matching

If your child can read, write each Spanish color word on an index card. Make another card with the corresponding color. Put all cards face down. Picking up one card at a time, try to match the color card with the Spanish word. When a match is found, put it aside. Continue until all of the cards have been matched.

Body Parts

ankle = tobillo

head = cabeza

hair = pelo/ cabello

eyes = ojos

nose = nariz

mouth = boca

tongue = lengua

teeth = dientes

neck = cuello

chest = pecho

shoulder = hombro

arm = brazo

elbow = codo

finger = dedo

fingernail = uña

stomach = estómago

navel = ombligo

leg = pierna

back = espalda

bottom = trasero

foot = pie

toe = dedo de pie

hand = mano

wrist = muñeca

Body Part Activities

Simple Pointing

A simple activity to practice the Spanish body part names is to sit down with your child and look at a stack of books. For each picture of a person or animal, ask your child to point to the character's eyes, mouth, feet, fingers, etc. Remember to also try and incorporate any other vocabulary that you have already studied such as numbers and colors by asking your child what color a body part is or how many of them there are.

Stickers

Give your child a sheet of stickers. Call aloud the name of a body part in Spanish and have your child place a sticker on the body part that you name. You can also have the child place the stickers on you or on a doll or stuffed animal. Reverse the game by asking the child to take the stickers off of each body part. If you have already studied colors, this game can gain an added dimension by telling the child what color sticker to place on which body part.

Body Part Art

Gather some old magazines, paper, scissors and a glue stick. With your child, look for and cut out one of each body part (a head, a neck, a nose, a mouth, some teeth, etc.). While you search for each part, make sure to repeat the name of each body part several times. Using as much Spanish as possible, say things like "I'm looking for a mouth" (*Busco una boca)* or "Do you like this mouth?" (*¿Te gusta esta boca?).* Ideally, all of the conversation surrounding the body parts would be in Spanish, but for now just concentrate on repeating the name of the body part at every opportunity, even if that means mixing your Spanish and English. Next, you and your child will build a person from the parts that you have cut out by pasting the parts together. It helps if you choose body parts that are similar in size. Talk about your picture together using the Spanish words for the body parts. Maximize repetition by sharing your artwork with another family member. This activity helps learners with varying learning styles to internalize the body part names.

Scary Monsters

If you have already studied colors and numbers with your child, this activity will help to review them while learning the body parts. Supply your child with some paper and crayons or markers to draw a monster that you will describe aloud. Tell your child how many of each body part to draw and what color it is, using as much Spanish as possible. For instance, you might say "He has one green eye" (*Tiene un ojo verde*). Try to make it as fun and silly as possible, giving the monster attributes like three yellow teeth or fifteen pink legs. Again, in an ideal world this activity would be conducted completely in Spanish, but your child will still benefit as long as you are using as many Spanish words as you know how to say.

Body Part Bingo

Bingo is one of those games that can be used with almost any vocabulary set. Clearly, this game is most fun with more than one person and when some sort of prize is involved, but can also be conducted with one child and no prizes. Draw a grid five spaces long and five spaces deep. In each space either draw or cut and paste a magazine picture of a body part by using the same method as in the Body Part Art activity above. Next, have your child use pennies or paper scraps to cover the pictures of the body parts that you call out in Spanish. When your child gets five in a row in any direction, he or she has a bingo. A printable bingo template is available on www.linguaculture.net.

Describing People

tall (boy) = alto

tall (girl) = alta

short (boy) = bajo (pronounced "BA-ho")

short (girl) = baja

thin (boy) = delgado

thin (girl) = delgada

fat (boy) = gordo

fat (girl) = gorda

handsome (boy) = bonito/ guapo

pretty (girl) = bonita/ guapa

ugly (boy) = feo

ugly (girl) = fea

nice (boy) = simpático

nice (girl) = simpática

mean (boy) = antipático

mean (girl) = antipática

light/fair/blond = rubio/a

dark/black or brown haired = moreno/a

red haired = pelirrojo/a

Grammar note:

Remember that masculine and feminine idea we talked about when we were learning color words? That applies here too. Make sure that your adjectives change to fit the gender and number of what they describe.

Describing People Activities

Describing Picture People

Sit down with your child with a magazine or stack of pictures and use Spanish description words for everyone that you see. When your child begins to catch on to some of the descriptions, you can ask your child, *"¿Cómo es?"* ("What is he/she like?") and see how much of the language he or she can produce. Keep practicing by describing people to your child that you see on television or in books and asking your child to describe people until the vocabulary comes naturally.

People Drawing

Give your child a set of crayons or markers and some paper. As you describe a person, have your child draw a person based on your description. For more fun, have two or more people participate and compare drawings.

Who am I?

Describe someone you know or a television character in Spanish and have your child guess who you are describing. Reverse roles and have your child describe someone for you to guess. Please note that it is most polite to reserve the negative adjectives for cartoon villains! This can also be a fun travel game.

Greetings and Goodbyes

Hello! =¡Hola!

How are you? = ¿Cómo estás?

Fine, thank you! = ¡Bien, gracias!

And you?= ¿Y tú?

Good morning = Buenos días.

Good afternoon =Buenas tardes.

Good night.=Buenas noches.

Goodbye!= ¡Adiós!

Greetings and Goodbyes Activities

Everyday Incorporation

Use your greetings and goodbyes at every opportunity throughout the day. In the car, when you see someone walking alongside the road, wave and say, *"¡Hola! ¿Cómo estás?"* or *"Buenos Días."* Greet your child in Spanish when he or she wakes up in the morning, or when he or she comes in from playing outside or returns from a visit with Grandma. You can even greet the household pet or your child's toys. The more your child hears the language in everyday settings, the quicker your child will learn the vocabulary.

Good Morning, Good Night!

With your child, turn out the lights and get in bed. Say, *"¡Buenas noches!"* Next, flip on the lights and say, *"¡Buenos días!"* Make it entertaining and silly. You can even pretend to snore when the lights are out. Continue for as long as your child finds this entertaining. This will help your child to learn the meaning of these common greetings in a natural and fun way.

Puppet Play

For puppet play, you will need a few stuffed animals or puppets. You can use toys that you already have, or you can increase the fun factor by making your own out of paper bags or old socks. Explain to your child that these puppets only speak Spanish. With the puppets, act out a greeting scene several times. Make the scene funny, using silly voices. You can make the most of all of the vocabulary by providing a backdrop. Draw a sunshine on one sheet of paper and a moon and stars on another and change the dialog to incorporate the appropriate greeting for the time of day. When you think your child has caught on, give him or her one of the puppets to help perform the scene with you. Encourage your child to play with the puppets alone later on with a reminder that they only speak Spanish. This will encourage pretend play in the foreign language and increase the time your child spends speaking Spanish on his or her own.

Introductions

What is your name? = ¿Cómo te llamas?

My name is ____ = Me llamo____

Nice to meet you!= ¡Mucho gusto!

Likewise= Igualmente.

Introductions Activities

Puppet Play

This is the same puppet activity that appears in the Greetings and Goodbyes section. This time, incorporate even more vocabulary into the dialog by including introductions. Give the puppets Spanish names. Have the puppets talk not only to one another, but to your child. Have the puppet ask your child what his or her name is and have the puppet express pleasure at meeting your child. Practice until the child has mastered the new vocabulary and, of course, encourage alone play with the Spanish speaking puppets for extra practice.

Picture People

Compile a stack of pictures of people or characters. Pictures can include family members, friends, cartoon characters or anyone that your child knows. Hold up the pictures and have the "people" introduce themselves to one another. Create funny combinations, like Elmo introducing himself to Grandpa. Change your voice for each person. You can have your child play the role of one person while you play the role of another or just have your child watch.

Real World Practice

It's time to take the show on the road. After practicing the introductions at home with family members and with the puppets, encourage your child to use the new vocabulary by introducing himself or herself to a native speaker. A likely place to find native speakers is at a local restaurant that serves cuisine from a Spanish speaking country.

Clothing

Belt = cinturón

Boots= botas

Bracelet = pulsera

Coat = abrigo

Dress= vestido

Earrings =aretes/ pendientes

Gloves= guantes

Hat= sombrero

High Heels = zapatos de tacón alto

Jacket = chaqueta

Pants= pantalones

Ring = anillo

Shirt = camisa

Shoes = zapatos

Shorts = pantalones cortos

Skirt= falda

Socks= calcetínes

Sweater= suéter

Tie= corbata

T-Shirt = camiseta

Underwear = ropa interior

Clothing Activities

Everyday Incorporation

Use the clothing words as often as possible in every day situations. Repeat the articles of clothing in Spanish as your child helps you fold the laundry, as you dress your child, as you are packing a suitcase or any other time you have the opportunity to use a clothing word.

Paper Dolls

Paper and felt dolls are a great way to reinforce clothing words. If you are artistic, you can make your own paper dolls by drawing or by cutting people and clothing from a magazine. If not, you can consider purchasing store bought kits or finding printable paper dolls on the Internet. Lay out each article of clothing for the doll and tell the child what clothing to put on the doll in Spanish. The crazier the combinations of clothing, the more entertaining the activity (think socks with high heeled shoes and underwear on the outside of the clothing). Reincorporate people description words by discussing what the doll looks like and what color the clothing is.

Fashion Show

People or dolls are dressed up for a Spanish fashion show. You and your child can take turns announcing the models and describing their outfits. Be sure to use your color words! Reincorporate meeting and greeting vocabulary by conducting a short interview with each model at the end of the runway. Greet the model appropriately for the time of day, ask the model what his or her name is and how they are doing and be sure to tell them that you are pleased to make their acquaintance. For further vocabulary reincorporation, give the models scores in Spanish on a scale from 0-10 based on how much you liked the outfit.

Packing

Pretend that you are going on a trip. Make a list in Spanish of the clothing items that you will need. You can stop at just making a list or you can actually fill a real suitcase as you name the items. Another option is to have your child draw pictures of the items on the list for your imaginary trip.

Food

Food descriptions
Bitter = amargo
Delicious = delicioso
Sweet = dulce
Sour = agrio
Tasty = sabroso
Yucky = guácala

Expressing Like or Dislike
I like...= Me gusta...
I don't like... = No me gusta...

Grammar note:
If you are talking about more than one thing, add an "n" to the end of gusta. For example, *Me gustan las uvas.*

Meal Times
Breakfast= desayuno
Lunch= almuerzo
Dinner = cena
Snack=merienda

General Food Categories
Fruit= fruta
Vegetables=verduras
Drink = bebida
Sweets= dulces
Meat= carne

Specific Food and Drink Names

Apple = manzana

Apple Juice = jugo de manzana, zumo de manzana

Banana = banana, plátano

Bread = pan

Butter = mantequilla

Cereal = cereales

Cheese = queso

Chicken = pollo

Cookie = galleta

Egg = huevo

Fries = patatas fritas

Grapes = uvas

Hamburger = hamburguesa

Milk = leche

Peanut Butter = crema de cacahuete

Toast = tostada

Water = agua

Food Activities

Everyday Incorporation

Use the Spanish food words as often as possible. Talk about the food while you cook, in the supermarket, when you see commercials on television, in restaurants and in the car. Use as much Spanish as you know when you are talking about the food, incorporating color and number words when you can. The more your child hears these words, the more they will be internalized. If you find it difficult to remember all of the vocabulary yourself, feel free to copy the words onto an index card to carry around with you as a cheat sheet.

Supermarket Scavenge

Make shopping for groceries a Spanish vocabulary game by naming something on your list in Spanish and having your child try to find it in the grocery store. See if your child can name foods that are not on your list as well. Talk about how the foods taste, whether you like them or not, what color they are and at what meal they are normally eaten. Consider buying your child a treat if he or she can name the item in Spanish. You'll be surprised how quickly children become proficient in Spanish when the possibility of getting some candy is on the line! Don't demand perfect pronunciation. The best policy where language is concerned is to reward your child even if you can only remotely understand him or her.

I like it, I don't like it

Cut out pictures of a variety of foods from magazines. On a large sheet of paper or poster board, draw a line down the center to divide the paper into *No me gusta* (I don't like it) and *Me gusta* (I like it) sections. Ask your child whether he or she likes each food item (*¿Te gusta?*) and paste each picture into the appropriate section. As you work with the pictures, be sure to talk about the foods in terms of flavor, color and at what meal they are normally eaten.

Food Hopscotch

With sidewalk chalk, draw or have your child draw pictures of a variety of foods. As you draw, take the opportunity to talk about the foods with the vocabulary that you know. Call out the name of a food and have your child try to jump to the drawing of that food without stepping on any other pictures. Adjust this game to your child's ability by drawing the food pictures closer together or farther apart.

Food Market

Using pictures of food cut from magazines, children's pretend food or real food from your cabinets, set up a small market in your child's play area. You and your child will take turns "shopping" in the market to practice food words and number words. Ask how much each item costs (*¿Cuánto cuesta?*) and use pretend money to buy the items. Make sure to talk about the items as much as possible with whatever vocabulary you know.

Recipes

Get a Spanish recipe from the Internet or a cookbook to try. This activity works best if you preview the recipes and choose one that has plenty of words that you already know. Be sure to have a dictionary on hand for looking up new words. Have your child help you figure out what the recipe says and talk about the foods in Spanish. Repeating this activity as often as possible with different recipes will build vocabulary and can quickly become a fun family ritual. Enhance the experience by taking your child shopping for the ingredients and doing the "Supermarket Scavenge" activity beforehand.

Holiday Food

Most holidays have specific foods that are associated with them. For instance, we associate pumpkin pie and turkey with Thanksgiving and candy canes and fruitcake with Christmas. Find out which foods are associated with whatever holiday you are focusing on with your child and find an authentic recipe to try. Try to incorporate whatever other vocabulary that you can as you cook and eat. See the holiday calendar in the culture section for more ideas.

Dinner Time

Objects

Chair = silla
Cup = taza
Fork = tenedor
Glass = vaso
Knife = cuchillo
Napkin = sirvilleta
Plate = plato
Spoon = cuchara
Table = mesa

Expressions

I need _____. = Necesito _____.
Thank you. = Gracias.
Will you pass the ____, please? = ¿Me pasas el/la _____, por favor?
More ____, please. = Más _____, por favor.

Dinner Time Activities

Everyday Incorporation

Every time you sit down at the table with your family, use your Spanish dinner time expressions and vocabulary. As you set and clear the table, talk about the different dishes and pieces of silverware. Ask your child to help you.

Puppet People

Have your puppet people attend a dinner. Let your child tell you what each puppet person needs (knife, fork, napkin, cup) as you set a table for them. Recycle previously learned vocabulary by having the puppet people converse about every possible subject that you have vocabulary for.

Dinner Time Drawing

Help your child draw a picture of a table. Talk about the items that should go on the table as you draw them. Recycle old vocabulary by discussing the colors and numbers of items.

Dinner Time Speed

This is a game played with two or more people. Cut out pictures of a napkin, table, chair, fork, spoon, etc. and spread them out on the floor or on a table an equal distance from the two players. You will call out the name of an object and both people will race to grab that picture first. For instance, you will say, *"Silla"*. Both players will try to grab the picture of the chair. The person who grabs that picture first will get to keep it. The person with the most pictures when all of the pictures are finally gone wins the game.

In the Restaurant

How many people? = ¿Cuántas personas?

Smoking or nonsmoking? = ¿Fumar o no fumar?

The check, please! = ¡La cuenta, por favor!

What would you like to drink? = ¿Qúe quisiera beber?

What would you like to order? = ¿Qúe quisiera pedir?

I'd like to order _____ = Me gustaría pedir ____.

More _____, please. = Más _____, por favor.

Thank you! = ¡Gracias!

You are welcome. = De nada.

Restaurant Activities

Everyday Incorporation

As often as possible, include vocabulary such as, *"por favor"*, *"De nada"* and *"Gracias"* in your everyday conversations. You probably already use these words with your child in English quite often. At mealtimes, ask your child what he or she would like to drink in Spanish. Practice *"¿Cuántas personas?"* by asking your child how many people there are in pictures from books, magazines or a family photo album.

Let's Play Restaurant!

With your child, make up some pretend menus. If your child can already write, you might write the words. Otherwise, you will probably want to draw or cut out pictures of food items. Talk about food in Spanish. Discuss color, taste, like or dislike and how much you think the price of the item should be to help review old vocabulary. Next, set up a table and act out a restaurant scene, taking turns being the waiter and customer. Make this activity more fun by dressing up in silly clothing or using funny voices.

Puppet People Restaurant

Using either the puppet people that you used for the previous vocabulary sets or some stuffed animals or dolls, use the new vocabulary to act out a restaurant scene. Recycle vocabulary by using four or more characters and pretending that at least two of them have never met one another before. Guide the conversation in a way that not only uses the new restaurant vocabulary but also reincorporates any older vocabulary that you might be able to work in.

Real World Practice

Take your child (or the entire family) to a local restaurant for some real life practice. Try to use a restaurant where you know that you will be served by a native speaker. Practice using as much Spanish as possible. Restaurant vocabulary is important and useful whether you are at home or abroad. Repeat this activity as often as possible until the language becomes second nature. Often, the native speakers that you meet will be more than happy to help you improve your Spanish. Real world practice is an invaluable key to language learning.

Verbs and Sentence Starters

Sentence Starters

I like ____. = Me gusta ____.

I want ____. = Quiero ____.

Do you like ____? = ¿Te gusta ____?

Do you want ____? = ¿Quieres ____?

I'm going to ____ = Voy a ____.

Are you going to ____? = ¿Vas a ____?

I have just ____. = Acabo de ____.

You have just ____. = Acabas de ____.

I have to ____. = Tengo que ____.

You have to____. = Tienes que ____.

Verbs

To Call = llamar (pronounced "YAH-mahr")

To Clean = limpiar

To Cook = cocinar

To Color = colorear

To Cut = cortar

To Dance = bailar

To Draw = dibujar (pronounced "DEE-boo-har")

To Drink = beber

To Eat = comer

To Find = encontrar

To Glue = pegar

To Go = ir

To Help = ayudar

To Hide = esconder

To Jump= saltar
To Mix = mezclar
To Play = jugar (pronounced "HOO-gar")
To Put = poner
To Speak = hablar
To Stop = parar
To Take = tomar
To Wait = esperar
To Work = trabajar (pronounced "tra-bah-HAR")
To Write = escribir

Grammar note:

The Spanish verbs above are given in infinitive form, which is the "to" form. For example, the verbs "to walk","to cook" and "to play" are all verbs in the infinitive form in English. You can combine the infinitives with the sentence starters above to form orations about all sorts of things:

Quiero ayudar. (I want to help)
Tienes que escribir. (You have to write)
Voy a colorear. (I am going to color)
¿Vas a jugar? (Are you going to play?)

To make a sentence negative, just say "no" at the beginning. For example:

No me gusta limpiar. I don't like to clean.
No voy a bailar. I'm not going to dance.
No tienes que esperar. You don't have to wait.

Verbs and Sentence Starter Activities

Everyday Incorporation

The possibilities for incorporating these sentence starters and verbs into your daily speech are endless. You can say, for example, "I have just cooked. Do you want to eat?, " "I'm going to clean. Do you want to help?" or "I'm going to go. Do you want to go?" Any time the opportunity presents itself, express what you have just done, are going to do, like, dislike or want in Spanish. This is a big chunk of vocabulary to digest at one time. Use those mnemonic devices that we talked about in the Frequently Asked Questions section and your *chuleta* (cheat sheet) to help you.

Story Time Embedding

Story Time embedding is good for the introduction of any new vocabulary. This is the same technique that was explained in the numbers activity section. As you tell your child his or her bedtime story, incorporate the new phrases in place of the English words whenever you can. Make the meaning of the vocabulary obvious from the context of the story.

Revisiting Old Activities

Consider revisiting any activities that you have done in the past that you and your child have enjoyed. This time incorporate the new vocabulary that you have learned. For instance, now you can try to speak in complete sentences throughout the entire process of cooking a Spanish recipe with your child. You can also revisit any of the activities that involved cutting, coloring and pasting and say things such as, "I'm not going to draw. You have to draw," or "Do you want to glue? I'm going to cut." Repeating activities with new vocabulary adds a whole new dimension to the experience. You will solidify previously learned vocabulary and see how far you and your child have come with the language.

Charades

Act out one of the verbs without speaking. Have your child guess in Spanish which verb you are acting out. When your child guesses correctly, swap places. If possible, enlist the participation of other friends or family members for more fun.

Verb Pictionary

With a note pad or erasable white board, choose a Spanish verb and begin to draw images that depict that word. Your child will try to guess which verb you are drawing. Swap places. This game is most fun played on teams with a group of people. On each team, take turns designating a drawer. Set a timer for one minute. The team has to guess the verb that the drawer is attempting to portray within that minute. If the correct verb has not been guessed by the end of that minute, the other team gets to guess.

Freestyle Puppet People

You have already established that your puppet people are Spanish-speaking toys. They have had many a Spanish adventure by now. It's time to expand their conversations to include full sentences with your new sentence starters and verbs. As always, guide the role play towards things that you know how to talk about in Spanish. You will be surprised how much you and your child can make these puppets say.

Prepositions

a = to, at, by means of

antes de = before

bajo= under

cerca de=near

con= with

de = of, from

delante de = in front of

dentro de = inside

después de = after

detrás de = behind

en= in, on

encima de = on top of

enfrente de = in front of

entre = between

fuera de= outside of

sobre = over, about

tras = after, behind

Preposition Activities

Everyday Incorporation

Prepositions are easy to incorporate into your normal conversation. Every object you come in contact with is either on top of, under, across from or beside something else! Using as much Spanish as possible, talk about the position of all sorts of objects. Tell your child that his or her lost toy is under the couch, that he or she should sit beside you, to put the toys in the basket, etc.

Sticker Book

Using either a children's reusable sticker book or just a sheet of interesting stickers and some old magazines, take turns telling one another where to place the sticker on each picture. For instance, put the butterfly sticker beside the flower or under the cloud. As always, speak as much Spanish as possible to include colors, numbers and other vocabulary.

Travel Hide and Seek

Travel hide and seek is a nice way to pass the time in the car or a waiting room. Pretend that you are only a few inches tall. Look around the room (or car) and decide where you would hide if you were tiny. Keep your location a secret. Your child will guess where you are hiding using Spanish prepositions and whatever household vocabulary he knows. For instance, let's say that you are hiding under the chair (*silla*). Your child will begin to guess your location:

"*¿Estás detrás de la mesa?*" (Are you behind the table?)

"*No...*"

"*¿Estás dentro de la taza?*" (Are you in the cup?)

"*No...*"

"*¿Estás debajo de la silla?*" (Are you under the chair?)

"*¡Sí! Ahora te toca a ti.*" (Yes! now it's your turn)

Chair Game

This game is most fun as a competition between two people. Both competitors have a teddy bear or stuffed animal and a chair. The two competitors are back to back so that they can't see one another. You call out the position of the bear and the competitors put the bear in that position. For instance, you might say "*El oso esta detrás de la silla*" (The bear is behind the chair). One person puts the bear in the correct position behind the chair. The other puts the bear on top of the chair. The correct individual gets a point. The first person to get 10 points wins.

Feelings and States of Being

Busy (female) = ocupada
Busy (male) = ocupado
Happy (female) = contenta/ alegre
Nervous (female) = nerviosa
Nervous (male) = nervioso
Sad (female or male) = triste
Sick (female) = enferma
Sick (male) = enfermo
Tired (female) = cansada
Tired (male) = cansado
Worried (female) = preocupada
Worried (male) = preocupado

Feelings and States of Being Activities

Feeling Collages

If you and your child enjoy making artwork, consider making a series of collages for each feeling or state of being that you study. For instance, take the word "busy." Go through magazines looking for pictures that depict the word "busy." You might find a picture of someone at a computer, someone raking leaves, cooking a meal, etc. As you look for the pictures, be sure to talk about them in Spanish with all of the vocabulary that you know. Additionally, be sure to mention the name for the state of being that you are working on as often as possible. Find ways to discuss other feeling words as well. For example, "Is she happy? No, she's sad." Take all of the pictures that you find and make a collage to display.

Drawing Feelings

On a white board, chalkboard or paper draw a stick person with a circle representing the face. Call out an emotion word in Spanish and have your child draw a face that goes along with what you are describing. Start over again with another word.

Gingerbread Men

Make some gingerbread men to decorate. Assemble lots of fun ingredients for decorating such as sprinkles, icing, sugar beads, licorice strands for hair, etc. For each gingerbread man or woman that you decorate, give your child instructions in Spanish for how he or she should look. Describe the emotion that should appear on the face, the color of the clothing, etc. When it comes time to eat the treats, have your child describe in Spanish which one he or she wants.

Charades

Without making a sound, act out a feeling or state of being. Your child will guess how you feel in Spanish. When your child guesses correctly, swap roles and let your child act out a feeling or state of being.

Family

Aunt = Tía
Brother = Hermano
Cousin (boy) = Primo
Cousin (girl) = Prima
Daughter = Hija
Father = Padre
Granddaughter = Nieta
Grandfather = Abuelo
Grandmother = Abuela
Grandson = Nieto
Great Grandmother = Bisabuela
Great Grandfather = Bisabuelo
Husband = Esposo
Mother= Madre
Nephew = Sobrino
Niece= Sobrina
Sister = Hermana
Son= Hijo
Stepfather=Padrastro
Stepmother = Madrastra
Uncle = Tío
Wife = Esposa

Family Activities

Family Photo Album

Look through a family photo album and talk about everyone you see. Use as many words as possible for each person. Take, for example, a picture of your child's grandmother. In addition to using the word grandmother, you can also mention that your child's grandmother is your mother, his or her grandfather's wife, his or her aunt or uncle's mother, and his or her great grandmother and great grandfather's daughter. Make the most of each photograph. Of course, also use any other Spanish that you can including people description words, color words and words for whatever other objects appear in the photographs.

Family Riddles

This is a handy car or travel game, especially for an older child who has a good grasp on the concept of family relations. For family riddles, you will ask your child to fill in the blank for statements such as the following:

La hermana de mi madre es mi ____.
The sister of my mother is my _____.

La madre de mi madre es mi ____.
My mother's mother is my _____.

La hija de mi tía es mi ____.
The daughter of my aunt is my _____.

El esposo de mi abuela es mi ____.
My grandmother's husband is my _____.

La esposa de mi tía es mi _____.
My uncle's wife is my _____.

El hijo de mi hermana es mi _____.
The son of my sister is my _____.

Guess That Family Member

For this game, you will recycle the people description words. You will describe a family member without using any names. For example, you might say that someone is "dark haired, short and nice." Your child will guess the family member, "My aunt? ... My sister?" until the correct family member is identified. This is also a good car or travel game to pass the time.

Family Tree

With a poster board, help your child make a family tree to display in the home. Cut out pictures of family members to paste in the correct location. Label the family members in Spanish. Make this project as fun as possible by adding decoration such as glitter, fall leaves or macaroni noodles. Use as many family, color and description words as possible while making the tree. Display the project in a prominent location and have your child explain the project to curious visitors using the Spanish family words.

Family Hop

Laminate some pictures of family members and tape them to the floor. Call out a family word such as "aunt." Your child will hop to the picture of his or her aunt. For older children, you can make the game more challenging by incorporating the family riddles. Call out, for example, "Your Aunt's son" to have your child hop on the photograph of a male cousin.

Around the House

Bathroom = Baño

Bed = Cama

Bedroom = Dormitorio

Chair = Silla

Closet = Armario

Door = Puerta

Hall = Pasillo

House = Casa

Kitchen = Cocina

Lamp = Lámpara

Living Room = Sala

Potty = Bacinica/ Orinal/ Retrete

Room = Cuarto

Shower = Ducha

Sink = Fregadero (kitchen)/ Lavabo (bathroom)

Sofa = Sofá

Table = Mesa

Tub = Bañera

Window = Ventana

Around the House Activities

Everyday Incorporation

Any time you have the opportunity, substitute the English household word for the Spanish. These very common words are easy to substitute. Tell your child to open or close the window or door, to place something on the table, to sit in the chair, etc.

Race Around the House

This is most fun with two or more competitors. Name a room or household object in Spanish. The two competitors race to the room or object and the first person to get there earns a point. The first person to earn 10 points wins the game.

Decorate with Stickers

Give your child some stickers and tell him or her in what room or on what object he can place them. For added practice, describe to your child which sticker can go where. For instance, tell your child that the blue sticker goes on the bed or that the sticker of the flower goes in the kitchen.

Dream House

Have your child draw a picture of a house. As your child draws, talk about the names of the rooms and household items in Spanish. Incorporate numbers by talking about how many of each item is in the picture and colors by talking about what color your child will draw each item. Keep the conversation going. Help your child label the items in Spanish.

Around the House Hop

On separate sheets of paper, have your child draw a picture

for each household word that you are studying. As your child draws, talk in Spanish about the item as much as possible. When finished, lay the pictures out on the floor. Say the word in Spanish and have your child hop to the correct picture. Sometimes it helps to attach the pictures to the floor with some tape. If you plan on repeating this activity often, consider having the pictures laminated.

Community

Apartment = apartamento/ piso
Church= iglesia
City = ciudad
Country (side) = campo
Farm = granja
Garden = jardín
House = casa
Library = biblioteca
Movie Theater = cine
Park= parque
Post Office = correo
Restaurant = restaurante
School = escuela
Store = tienda
Supermarket = supermercado
Zoo = zoológico

Community Activities

Everyday Incorporation

Any time you can, incorporate the Spanish name of whatever place you are talking about into your conversations with your child. As you drive past places in your car, name them in Spanish. If you see a picture of a place you know how to say in a book or magazine, mention it aloud in Spanish. Let your child hear the vocabulary as often as possible.

Model Community

Build a model community out of things that you have lying around the house. You can make the base out of some cardboard or an old piece of poster board. The ground can be made to look realistic by smearing glue on the base and sprinkling dirt or dried parsley on top of it for dirt or grass. Buildings and other constructions can be made from cardboard, empty boxes, straws, popsicle sticks, toothpicks, buttons, empty paper towel rolls, cocktail umbrellas, modeling clay and old or broken toys. Be creative! A burned out light bulb can double for a water tower and cinnamon sticks make excellent tree trunks. As you construct your community, use as much Spanish as you can-especially vocabulary related to the community. Label the locations if you would like by making small signs attached to toothpicks stuck into balls of modeling clay.

Puppet People

If your model community is big enough, let your puppet people play out a scene in the community. By now, your puppet people have a lot of vocabulary to work with, so be creative with the story lines. Be sure to have the puppet people visit every possible location in the community and repeat those words as many times as you can. Maybe the puppet people are looking for something important and have to go to everywhere in the community to see if it is hidden there. If your normal puppet people are too big for this activity, try using something like action figures.

Community Map

On a large sheet of butcher paper or with sidewalk chalk, help your child draw a map of your community. Draw the buildings, parks and streets. Make the streets big enough for your child to walk on. Talk about the locations in Spanish as you draw. Label them if you would like. Once you have completed the drawing, have your child "go" to the locations that you call out by walking down the streets that you have created. Swap places and let your child tell you where on the map you should go. If you have drawn your map on butcher paper, be sure to save it for a future activity about direction words.

Directions

Address= Dirección

Around here= por aquí

Can you tell me how to get to _____? = ¿Como llego a_____?

If you see ____, you've passed it= Si ve _____, se ha pasado.

Go straight = Siga recto./Siga derecho.

Left= izquierda

Pass ____. = Pasa ____.

Right= derecha

Sign= letrero/ señal

Straight= derecho

Stop = alto/ pare

Stop light= semáforo

Take a right= Vaya a la derecha

Take a left= Vaya a la izquierda

Where is ____?= ¿Dónde está _____?

Direction Activites

Everyday Incorporation

Any time you have the opportunity, use the Spanish direction words. If your family is in the car and your spouse is driving, give him or her directions in Spanish to where you are going, even if he or she already knows how to get there. As you walk or drive with your child, describe what direction that you are going in Spanish. Once your child catches on to the vocabulary, ask him or her the way to get to the park, to school, etc. Use the words as often as you can.

Community Model or Map

Either recycle the community model that you and your child made, use the large map that you drew or make a new model or map of a real or imaginary place. Using your puppet people, action figures or having your child walk directly on a large map, take turns giving and taking directions to different places in the community. Be sure to practice your community words as well!

Taxi

Make a city out of your house, a place on your driveway or other area using signs, chalk or tape. For instance, an office might be the library, the kitchen might be a restaurant, etc. In your driveway or an empty parking lot, simply draw streets and buildings with sidewalk chalk. In a garage or carport, either draw with chalk or lay down colored electrical tape for streets. Using a wagon or rolling office chair, play "taxi" with your child. The child will have to give you, the taxi driver, directions to where he or she wants to go. You will push your child in the rolling chair, following the directions that he or she gives you. If you wish, swap places with your child. Most children love this game.

Weather and Seasons

Seasons

Spring= Primavera

Summer = Verano

Fall= Otoño

Winter= Invierno

Weather

It's cloudy = Está nublado

It's cold= Hace frío

It's hot= Hace calor

It's raining= Llueve

It's snowing= Nieva

It's sunny= Hace sol

It's windy= Hace viento

The weather is good= Hace buen tiempo

The weather is bad= Hace mal tiempo

Weather= Tiempo

What is the weather like? = ¿Cómo está el tiempo?

Weather Activities

Everyday Incorporation

Talk about the weather at every opportunity. Mention the temperature often. If possible, watch a weather report on Spanish television. Talk about the seasons and typical weather for each season. Look at books, magazines and family photographs and talk about what the weather is like in each scene. Give your child plenty of comprehensible input to help him or her become proficient at describing the condition of his environment in Spanish.

Puppet People

With your child's help, create a collection of drawings depicting different weather situations. While you make these drawings, be sure to talk about the weather in Spanish as much as possible . Make one of your puppet people a weatherman and use your pictures as a backdrop. The puppet weatherman should give the forecast that goes along with each picture. For older children, incorporate geography by drawing a map of a Spanish-speaking country and placing pictures such as a snowflake, a sunshine or a rain cloud on certain cities. Your puppet person can give the forecast for each city appearing on the map.

Paper Dolls

Use the same paper dolls that you used during the clothing activities. This time, you will describe what the weather is like and your child will dress the paper doll appropriately for the weather. Take turns. Recycle previous vocabulary by talking about the clothing in Spanish as much as possible.

Weather Bingo

Using the bingo template that we have used for other vocabulary activities (5 spaces across and 5 spaces down), have your child draw a symbol for a different weather situation in each space. Some of the situations may have to be repeated to fill all of the blanks. This is fine. You will call out what the weather is like. Your child will find the corresponding picture on his bingo card and mark it off. If he has two of the same picture, he will choose which one to mark off. For instance, if you say, "*Hace sol*" and your child has three sunshines drawn on his card, he will pick only one sunshine to cross off. When he has made a straight line down, across or diagonally, he has a bingo.

Days and Months

Months of the Year

January = Enero
February = Febrero
March = Marzo
April = Abril
May = Mayo
June = Junio
July = Julio
August = Agosto
September = Septiembre
October = Octubre
November = Noviembre
December = Diciembre

Days of the Week

Sunday = Domingo
Monday = Lunes
Tuesday = Martes
Wednesday = Miércoles
Thursday = Jueves
Friday = Viernes
Saturday = Sábado

Days and Months Activities

Name that Day or Month

Talk about the days of the week and months of the year. Ask your child on what days or during what months you and your family does certain activities and have your child answer you in Spanish. Use as much related Spanish as you can. Additionally, ask your child about which holidays are celebrated during which months. Ask your child to tell you what month his or her birthday is in, what month you normally go on vacation, what month Christmas is in, which night of the week you normally go out for ice cream or to worship, etc.

Year Book

For each month of the year, help your child to draw a picture representing what he or she associates each month with. For example, the month of August might be associated with a return to school. Your child might draw a schoolhouse, pencils, books and a desk. Talk about the colors and pictures that your child is drawing in Spanish. While he or she draws, be sure to mention the Spanish word for the month that you are working on as many times as possible. Write the Spanish name of the month above each picture that represents the month. Put it in a report folder or binder to display.

Holiday Calendar

Help your child make a Spanish calendar. You can draw your own with a ruler and pen or you can use a computer program to make one. Have your child help you remember the names of the months, days of the week and the numbers in Spanish to label on the calendar. Label all of the Spanish holidays that you know. Display the calendar in your home. Each time you learn about a new holiday, write it on the calendar. You can use the holiday calendar in the culture section as a reference. Try and discover as much about each holiday as you can with your child by reading through cultural books, looking at Internet sites and by talking to native speakers. For each new holiday, draw a symbol on the calendar to help you remember what the holiday is all about.

Animals and Insects

ant = hormiga
bear = oso
bee = abeja
bird = pájaro
bull = toro
butterfly = mariposa
cat = gato
chicken = pollo
cockroach = cucaracha
cow = vaca
crocodile = cocodrilo
dog = perro
duck = pato
elephant = elefante
fish= pez
fly = mosca
fox = zorro
frog = rana
giraffe = jirafa
goat = cabra
hen = gallina
horse = caballo
lion = león

lizard = lagarto

mouse = ratón

octopus = pólipo/ pulpo

pig= cerdo

rabbit = conejo

shark = tiburón

sheep = oveja

snail = caracol

snake = serpiente

spider = araña

squirrel = ardilla

swan = cisne

tiger = tigre

turkey = pavo

turtle = tortuga

whale = ballena

wolf= lobo

zebra = cebra

Animals and Insects Activities

Clay Animals

Get some multicolored modeling clay or dough. Name an animal or insect in Spanish and help your child make the animal from clay. Make them as detailed as possible and use the project as an opportunity to repeat the animal and insect words as well as to recycle old vocabulary as you describe them. Once your mini clay zoo is assembled, have your child present the zoo to another family member, naming each animal in Spanish.

Cucaracha

Make two identical sets of index cards with pictures of all of the animals and insects on them. You could print pictures from the Internet, cut them from pictures or simply draw them. Make one extra card with a picture of a cockroach on it (*cucaracha*). Shuffle all of the cards together and deal them. If you have a pair of animals in your set, match them and put them on the table. You want to make a match for every animal, so ask your child if he or she has a match to a card you have by asking "*¿Tienes _____?*". If your child has the card, he or she will give it to you, you will pair the two cards and set them on the table. If not, you will draw a card from your child's hand without looking at the cards. Next, it will be your child's turn to ask you if you have a certain animal. Continue in this manner until all of the cards have been matched. The person left with the *cucaracha* card loses. In case you have not noticed, this game is played like the game Old Maid.

Jungle Book

Draw, print or cut pictures of animals and compile them in a sort of picture dictionary. As you make the dictionary, discuss the animals in Spanish. Help your child label the animals. When you are finished with the dictionary, have your child present the book in Spanish to a family member. Display the book in your home.

A Trip to the Zoo

Take a trip to the zoo with your child. Speak as much Spanish as you can for the duration of the trip. Discuss the animals in Spanish. Use colors and numbers. If your zoo has brochures and maps in Spanish, use them. Have your child help you look at the zoo map and use the direction words that he or she has learned to tell you how to get to the exhibits. Use food words when it is time to eat lunch. Fill the day with Spanish.

Part III
Teaching Culture

Introduction to Teaching Culture

Students often assume that for each Spanish word, there is an exact equivalent in English. However, as a former professor of mine used to be fond of repeating, "Spanish is not English with Spanish words." Spanish really is a completely different language. The same word in Spanish and English can have very different connotations. Take, for example, the word "obvious." "Obvious" is a normal English word, used by people of every education level. If you look up "obvious" in an English-Spanish dictionary, you will see the word *obvio*. If you look up *obvio* in a Spanish dictionary, you will find that the definition is the same as the English word "obvious." And why wouldn't it be? It's a cognate. However, when I was a college student in Spain, I got strange reactions when I used this word. The standard reaction was a sort of smirk and the reply, "Wow, you speak better Spanish than me." It seems that in Spain, using the word *obvio* makes one sound pretentious and more or less like you just emerged from the pages of some dusty old tome. No dictionary will tell you this. And just try it and see what kind of reaction you get when you literally translate an idiomatic expression such as "it costs an arm and a leg" or "she's got some money to burn". Spanish truly is not English with Spanish words. In the same way, Spanish culture is not Spanish traditions with American people. Every culture in the world is truly, deeply different with different value systems that drive the behaviors and customs. It is just as important to learn culture as it is to learn language. You can learn the words to the Spanish language, but if you do not learn the culture, you will be unable to function.

What is culture? Many people think of culture as a country's food, customs and art forms. There is an idea that people around the world are basically the same- it's just that we eat different foods, have different schedules, we dress differently and our buildings and monuments don't look alike. We assume that most of our reactions and thoughts are universally experienced, when in actuality, we are just viewing things through the filter of our own enculturation.

This filter is called a "schema." A schema is all of the background knowledge that we have about something. We have a schema for everything we know about and we process every new experience through our schemata. We take what we already know and fill in the gaps with new information. When our brain chooses what schema through which to filter new information, this is known as "instantiation." For instance, an exchange student in a foreign situation who finds himself in a classroom where he understands nothing automatically instantiates a classroom schema. Everything he experiences is filtered through the schema that his mind tells him to expect based on his prior experience in classrooms. A learner working through this classroom schema might assume that when the teacher is calling roll, the word that the students keep saying in response is "here" or "present." This learner is using his schema to make assumptions and fill in gaps of understanding. The problem is that many of our schemata are culture-bound. Maybe in this particular culture, people do not say "here" when the teacher calls roll. For all this learner knows, the students could be saying "potato." In this imaginary culture, potatoes are considered sacred and are a symbol of wisdom. To symbolize the importance of wisdom, the school provides a potato for each student at break each day. This is standard in every public school in this imaginary culture. At the beginning of the day, the teacher calls out a student's name, and the student is to answer "potato" if he or she will accept the potato for that day so that the school will know how many potatoes to cook.

Based on his U.S.A. classroom schema, our imaginary learner has now stored the word "potato" in his memory where the word "here" or "present" should be- a situation that is bound to elicit confusion later on when his host mother asks him if he wants a potato. This problem was caused because the learner did not have a classroom schema in place for in the target culture and had to default to the classroom schema of his own culture. We need to learn more about the target culture so that we can begin to build a schema for the situations that we might encounter and subsequently instantiate the correct schema.

When I was a student in Seville, I noticed that nothing seemed to happen according to schedule. Nobody ever showed up to open the school on time, the buses were constantly on strike and nobody seemed to even care that it was making them late for school and work! If I made a date with a friend, it was nothing for them to show up half an hour to one hour late. Filtering these experiences through the schema of my own culture, the Spanish people seemed a little irresponsible. After all, in the United States we are very fast-paced and making someone wait is one of the most inconsiderate things that one can do. Time is money, right? Nobody had explained to me that Spanish culture and the culture of the United States actually have completely different ways of looking at the concept of time. Spain (and Seville in particular) operates on something called polychronic time.

Polychronic cultures view time differently. For them, time is very fluid. Schedules are not rigid, interruptions are expected and plans change often. To a person in a polychronic mindset, having to wait an hour for someone who is late to a meeting might be seen as a welcome opportunity to get a cup of coffee at a nearby café. When one activity is upset, the polychron simply moves on to another.

The United States operates on monochronic time. Monochronic time is very structured and rigid. Everything is scheduled down to the minute and precautions are taken to guard against interruptions. When unavoidable interruptions occur, they are normally met with a sense of stress and panic, as this throws off the schedule of everything else. That which makes the monochron's blood boil is taken in stride by the polychron. In a polychronic culture, clock time is seen as arbitrary and in a monochronic culture every activity is ruled by the clock.

Having only ever experienced monochronic cultures (the United States and Germany), I had no idea that polychronic time even existed. I filtered everything that occurred through the schema of monochronic time, thinking that my own culture's attitude regarding time was universal. The very concept of polychronic time is difficult to grasp for people who have only been exposed to a monochronic culture. "How do they ever get anything done?" we wonder. Amazingly, they do! I'm still not sure how it happens. If I had come to Spain with an established schema for a polychronic culture, I would not have been nearly as shocked that the one hour photo took an *entire day*.

Learning culture so that our brains can instantiate the correct schema for our experience is crucial in order to truly function within the target culture. Just learning language is simply not enough. The deeper we go toward understanding the values and themes which underly culture, the more effectively we can function and communicate. A value is a concern that a culture holds important. A theme is a value that is so important in the culture that it permeates the behavior patterns across the board. What people normally think of as culture such as food, clothing and art forms are merely outward symbols of these underlying values and themes. Analyzing deep culture goes beyond memorization of trivia into a true understanding of how a culture works from the inside.

In one culture, something that is highly valued might be considered unimportant or frivolous in another. Our American value on independence that drives children to leave the home at 18 years of age might be considered ridiculous in a culture where generations live in the same household. Similarly, the "American dream" of owning one's own home is a result of cultural conditioning. Our culture values success as a result of hard work and owning our own home is a sign that we have worked hard enough to deserve our success. The fact that our country has ample space for everyone to own a home is also a factor. We are culturally conditioned to respond to our need for shelter by buying our own homes if we are financially able instead of continuing to live at home with our families.

Cultural schemata also determine what mental images are evoked when we hear a word. For instance, if someone says the word "house," a Guatemalan will have a very different mental image attached to that word than someone from the United States. There are many words that are culture bound in this manner. Take, for instance, the word "milk." To us, milk comes either in a carton or a plastic jug. Milk is kept refrigerated and is served cold. In Spanish, the word for milk is *leche*. In Spain, *leche* is bought in a box that is kept in the pantry. It is served room temperature and has a sweet aftertaste that fresh milk does not carry. So are the Spaniard and the American having a conversation about milk really talking about the same thing?

Other examples of culture-bound words are *tortilla* and *taco*. Both are words which change meanings drastically depending through what cultural schema you are filtering information. When people in the Americas hear the word *tortilla*, we generally think of a very thin flour or corn pancake, because that is what the word signifies in the cultures that we have the most experience with. However, the American traveler in Spain with no existing cultural schema for the country ordering a *tortilla* is going to be surprised with a type of omelet with potatoes, onions or mushrooms. That same traveler is going to be met with amusement if he tries to order a *taco*, because in Spain, a *taco* is a curse word. Part of teaching culture is to help students build a schema for the target country that will allow the words and mental images evoked by those images to coincide.

The culture activities presented in this section are meant to help your child to begin constructing a schema for the target culture(s). The activities here are not geared toward any specific culture. That choice will be up to you. You can focus your instruction on a specific culture or you can touch on several, depending on what you feel is most beneficial for your child. If you are planning a trip to a specific country, I would suggest that you focus most of your attention on that culture so that you and your family will get the most out of the experience.

For each activity, I cannot stress enough the importance of using culturally authentic images and texts. Your child will be using the images in the activities that you conduct to build his or her schema for the target culture. Your child will be learning culture indirectly through the materials that you provide, so make sure that your materials are culture rich.

Above all, strive to promote a positive attitude toward the target culture- an attitude free of judgment. Attempt to dig deep into the culture to understand the values and themes that drive the culture and try to analyze what you find from the target culture's perspective. This will help to trigger a lifelong interest for the language and culture that will continue to benefit your child throughout the years.

Holidays

Every country has holidays that are specific to its particular culture. Many world traditions are encapsulated in the celebration of holidays and festivals, so making a study of the holidays of the Spanish-speaking world can be a fabulous way to examine the target cultures. Below, you will find a chronological listing of the major holidays in the Spanish-speaking world along with a very brief description of each holiday. Below the description of the most well-known holidays, you will find useful vocabulary and accompanying activities to help you make the most of your study. Remember that you should make these activities as much about having fun and cultivating a positive attitude toward the target culture as they are about learning the facts surrounding the celebrations.

In addition to or in lieu of the suggested activities, consider an extensive holiday research project on any one holiday that you choose. Find out as much as you can about the holiday by looking at books, watching movies or through Internet research. Travel guides can be a good source of information on foreign holidays. There are also children's books available for most holidays that help to explain the customs in simplified language. Any time you come across an interesting picture, copy it and cut it out, print it or draw it yourself. Compile pictures, recipes and other useful information in a three ring binder or on a poster board to display. Try the recipes that you find, listen to the music and replicate any of the customs that you find interesting. Create crafts that go along with the holiday and display them. Find a native speaker and interview him or her about the holiday. Use all of the Spanish that you have learned any time you are working on the project and try to pick up as much new vocabulary as possible! If you have started a language group with friends, get together as a group and celebrate each holiday. This is an excellent way to acquire new vocabulary and to help to build a schema for the target culture. If you and your child enjoy the holiday studies, you can continue to expand on these projects year after year.

Holiday Calendar of the Spanish Speaking World

January

January 1 – New Year
A public holiday in all Spanish speaking countries. See December 31 for activities surrounding the New Year.

January 6- Three Kings Day
Three Kings Day or *Los Reyes Magos* is celebrated on January 6. In Spain, this holiday is even more important than Christmas. It involves the exchanging of gifts, parades and other festivities.

Three Kings Vocabulary
Candy= caramelos
Gifts= regalos
Parade= cabalgata
Three Kings Day = Los Reyes Magos

Three Kings Activities
Look up pictures of *Los Reyes Magos* celebrations and find out as much as you can about the holiday. Talk about the holiday with your child. Your family might exchange small gifts for Three Kings Day. Look up a recipe for Three Kings Bread (*Roscón de Reyes*) on the Internet or in a Spanish cookbook and cook it with your child. Share the bread with your family along with some hot chocolate.

Draw a picture of the Three Kings or dress up some dolls or stuffed animals as the Three Kings in honor of the holiday. If you feel very inspired, gather a few friends, dress up as the Three Kings and pass out gifts.

Jan 10- Eugenio María de Hostos Birthday
In Puerto Rico, the birthday of this literary and political figure is celebrated.

January 20- Saint Sebastian Day
San Sebastián is celebrated in Spain each year, especially in the Basque City of San Sebastián. There are festivities such as street parties, dancing and bullfighting.

January 21 - Feast of Our Lady of Highest Grace
In the Dominican Republic, the Feast of *Nuestra Sra. De Altagracia*, the patron virgin of the Dominican Republic is celebrated.

January 26 - Juan Pablo Duarte Day
This holiday is celebrated each year in the Dominican Republic in honor of Juan Pablo Duarte, who helped free the Dominican Republic from Haiti.

January 28 - José Martí Birthday
The Birthday of José Martí is celebrated in Cuba. José Martí was a famous literary figure and political activist.

José Martí Activity
If your child is interested, look up information about José Martí and share it with your child. Show your child where Cuba is on the map and look up pictures of Cuba. Discuss and draw pictures about what you see. Look up and prepare a Cuban dish and listen to some Cuban

music. Draw or sew a Cuban flag and add it to your flag collection.

February

February (movable holiday) - *Carnaval*
Carnaval is a movable holiday that is celebrated before Ash Wednesday each year. This festival is celebrated in Spain and in Central and South America. *Carnaval* corresponds with our Mardi Gras celebrations and often involves a street party and elaborate costumes.

Carnaval Vocabulary
Costume = disfraze
Fish= pescado
Choir= coro
Music= música

Carnaval Activity
Look up pictures of a *Carnaval* celebration. The celebration of *Carnaval* varies from country to country, but the most elaborate festival takes place in Cádiz, Spain. Let your child choose a costume to wear or let him or her have a costume party with friends.

February 2- Candlemas
La Candelaria, or Candlemas, is celebrated each year in various Spanish-speaking countries around the world. This celebration commemorates the restoration of the ceremonial cleanliness of the Holy Virgin after the birth of Jesus. In many cases, *Candelaria* is celebrated with parades and parties.

February 2 – Treaty of Guadalupe Hidalgo
This treaty marked the end of the Mexican War.

February 3 – Festival of San Blas

La Fiesta de San Blas is a public holiday in Paraguay to honor its patron saint.

February 21 - Benito Juárez Birthday

In Mexico, Benito Juárez's birthday is celebrated as a public holiday. Benito Juárez was president twice.

February 24 – Mexican Flag Day

Mexico celebrates Flag Day in February of each year. This is similar to Flag Day in the United States.

Flag Day Activity

Look up a picture of the Mexican flag. Discuss the symbols and colors and make a flag to display. Consider cooking an authentic Mexican meal and using the flag as a centerpiece.

February 26 – Aberri Eguna

Aberri Eguna is National Day for the Basque country of Spain.

February 27 – Dominican Republic Independence Day

This holiday commemorates the Dominican Republic's Independence from Haiti.

March

March 12-19 – *Las Fallas*

In Spain, the celebration of *Las Fallas* takes place each year in Valencia. All year, groups work on elaborate carnival figures, which can sometimes be as tall as a building. The figures are paraded through the streets and judged. The festival culminates with a fireworks display and the burning of the figures. Firefighters are always nearby to keep the fires from getting out of control. This is one of the most popular Spanish festivals.

Las Fallas Vocabulary

Burn = quemar
Carnival Figures= cabezudos
Fire = fuego
Fireworks= fuegos artificiales

Las Fallas Activities

If you have satellite television, watch footage of *Las Fallas*, which is normally widely covered on Spanish channels. Otherwise, you might find a video at a local library. Construct a mini *cabezudo* with your child from materials that you find around the house. If you wish, burn it afterwards (taking the proper safety precautions, of course). Depending on the laws in your area, you might even consider shooting fireworks.

March 21 – Benito Juárez Birthday

In Mexico, the birth of Benito Juárez, a military leader, is celebrated.

March 22 – Emancipation Day

Emancipation Day is celebrated in Puerto Rico to commemorate the freeing of the slaves in 1873.

April

April (movable holiday) – Easter Week

The Holy Week festival or *Semana Santa* begins on Palm Sunday and culminates on Easter. Easter is a movable holiday which is observed on the first Sunday that falls after the full moon after the equinox. In

Spain and in some parts of Central and South America, this festival is celebrated by decorating pasos, or floats that travel throughout the city. The most elaborate *Semana Santa* celebration takes place in Seville, Spain. This very complicated and fascinating holiday has its own style of music, food and dress associated with it.

Holy Week Vocabulary

Brotherhood = hermandad

Crowd = bulla

Floats= pasos

Holy Week = Semana Santa

Nazarenes = nazarenos

Procession = procesión

Semana Santa Activities

There are many recipes specific to *Semana Santa*. These foods will vary depending on what country you happen to be focusing on. Choose one and try it. The most famous *Semana Santa* celebration takes place in Seville, Spain. During Holy Week in Seville, the streets smell of orange blossoms and Jasmine. Light a jasmine candle or brew some jasmine tea and keep some fresh oranges on hand to create the mood. Watch some processions on the Internet or on television. Draw a picture of or build your own paso from things that you have lying around the house like an old shoe box or artificial flowers. If you want to study Seville's *Semana Santa* in depth, try visiting http://www.semana-santa.org/, the official site of the Holy Week festivities. Anything you ever wanted to know about *Semana Santa* is there along with plenty of pictures, music and video. Just be ready to break out the dictionary, because it is in Spanish!

April (movable holiday) – April Fair

Spain celebrates the *Feria de Abril* one week after Easter in Seville.

Families and companies set up public and private tents and celebrate. Many people dress in traditional attire and dance *sevillanas*, which is a four part dance loosely associated with flamenco. Men and women on horseback flood the city for a week of celebration.

Feria Vocabulary

Lantern = faro
Horse = caballo
Regional Dance of Seville = Sevillanas

Feria Activities

Try to find a dance class in your area that offers *sevillanas*. If there is nothing in your area, look for an instructional DVD or video. *Sevillanas* is danced to a certain type of music- find some *sevillanas* to listen to even if you don't learn the dance. Each year, a new *Feria* poster is released. Try looking at some of the old posters and then create your own with your child. Look on the Internet or in a recipe book for some tapas to prepare. Decorate a room with some paper lanterns and the posters that you created, put on some music and invite some friends over to learn *sevillanas* and eat tapas.

April 11 – Battle of Rivas Day

In Costa Rica, the Battle of Rivas is commemorated.

April 14 – Independence Day

In Paraguay, *La Día de la Independencia* is a public holiday.

April 19 – Patriot's Day

In Uruguay, April 19 celebrates the anniversary of the landing of the 33 exiles.

April 23 – *San Jordí*

In Northern Spain, this day is celebrated in honor of Catalonia's patron saint. It is customary for the women and men to exchange gifts of books and flowers on this day.

May

May 1 – Labor Day
Día del Trabajo is a public holiday across the Spanish speaking world.

May 5 – *Cinco de Mayo*
Cinco de Mayo is celebrated in Mexico to commemorate the victory of Puebla against the French. It is often mistakenly thought of as Mexican Independence Day (that's actually September 16).

Cinco de Mayo Activity
Research how *Cinco de Mayo* is celebrated in Mexico. If possible, ask a native speaker to talk about his or her experiences regarding *Cinco de Mayo*. The easiest way to do this is to visit an authentic Mexican restaurant on the holiday and talk to the waiters or owners. Compare and contrast how *Cinco de Mayo* is celebrated here in the United States vs. in Mexico.

May 10 – Day of the Mothers
Día de las Madres is observed to honor mothers in Mexico and other parts of the Spanish speaking world.

May 15 – Independence Day
Independence Day for Paraguay is celebrated on this date each year.

May 18 – Battle of Las Piedras

Paraguay celebrates the 1828 end to conflict between Uruguay and Brazil.

May 25 – *Día de la Patria*

Argentina celebrates the *Revolución de Mayo* in remembrance of this day in 1810.

May (movable holiday) – *El Rocío*

In Spain, *El Rocío* is a movable festival celebrated one week before Pentecost Monday. Nearly one million people make a pilgrimage to visit Spain's most beloved virgins- *La Virgin del Rocío*. Entire streets shut down as oxen-drawn wagons make their way south. The festival culminates with the emergence of the *Virgin del Rocío* from her home in the church.

El Rocío Vocabulary

Pilgrimage = romería
Dance = bailar
Pray =rezar
Jump = saltar

El Rocío Activities

Look for pictures and video footage of this event. Draw pictures about what you see. Talk about what it might be like to participate in the pilgrimage. Plan a short pilgrimage of your own to personalize the information.

June

June (movable holiday) – Corpus Christi

Corpus Christi is celebrated about nine weeks after Easter. It is observed in most Spanish speaking countries as a Catholic holiday designed to celebrate the Eucharist. The celebration of Corpus Christi often involves a solemn procession.

June 19 – Artigas Day
In Uruguay, this holiday marks the birthday of José Gervasio Artigas, an important figure in the history of Uruguay.

June 20 – Flag Day
Argentina's *Día de la Bandera* is celebrated as a public holiday.

June 24 – Feast of Saint John
The holiday of San Juan is celebrated in many parts of the Catholic world. Its celebration traditionally involves jumping over or walking through fires. In Puerto Rico, this holiday is particularly meaningful because it remembers the patron saint of San Juan.

June 29 – Peter and Paul Day
San Pedro y San Pablo is celebrated across the Spanish speaking world.

July

July 5 – Independence Day
This is Venezuela's Independence Day.

July 6-14 – *San Fermín* (The Running of the Bulls)
This very popular festival takes place each year in Pamplona, Spain. Bulls are released into the streets and the men run with them. People who grow up with this tradition learn special ways to keep themselves safe. This festival draws crowds of tourists each year. This festival is to remember the patron saint of the city being put to death by being

dragged by bulls.

Running of the Bulls Vocabulary

Bull = toro

Inury = herida

Run = correr

Street = calle

Running of the Bulls Activities

The run takes place each year along the same route. Look up the route and draw a map of it. This event is often televised, even on American television. Watch the event on television and see if you can follow it on your map. Discuss this event with your child, using as much Spanish as possible. Notice how the people are dressed and what the buildings look like. Discuss similarities and differences in what you see and what you would see at an event in your own culture.

July 9 – Independence Day

This day is Independence Day for Argentina.

July 19 – Revolution Day

In Nicaragua, this holiday celebrates the declaration of victory over the Somoza dictatorship.

July 20 – Independence Day

This is Independence Day for Colombia.

July 24 - Simón Bolivar's Birthday

The birthday of Simón Bolivar is observed to celebrate his help in the independence of Bolivia, Colombia, Ecuador, Peru and Venezuela.

July 25 - *Fiesta de Santiago*

The Feast of St. James, the patron saint of Spain, is a beloved holiday in Europe. Thousands of people make a pilgrimage to Santiago de Compostela in the week leading up to this day to take part in the festivities of this religious holiday.

July 26 - Revolution Day
Cuba celebrates Revolution Day on this day each year.

July 28 - Independence Day
Día de la Independencia is celebrated in Peru on this day.

August

August 1-6 – Feast of the Savior of the World
El Salvador del Mundo is celebrated in El Salvador. This is a festival for the patron saint of El Salvador. There are street parties and music.

August 6 - Independence Day
Bolivia's *Día de la Independencia*.

August 7- Battle of *Boyacá*
In Colombia, this public holiday commemorates a battle in which the Spanish were defeated.

Aug 10 - Independence Day
This is the day that Ecuador celebrates *Día de la Independencia*.

August 15 - Feast of the Assumption
This holiday is popular throughout the Spanish-speaking world as a celebration of the Holy Virgin's ascent into heaven.

August 17 - San Martín Day
This holiday honors the death of José Francisco de San Martín and is celebrated in Argentina.

Aug 25 - Independence Day
Uruguay celebrates *Día de la Independencia* on this day.

September

Sept. 8 - Feast of Nuestra Señora de la Caridad del Cobre
This holiday is observed in Cuba to honor the patron of Cuba.

September 11- National Day of Catalonia
Día Nacional de Cataluña is observed in Catalonia each year on this day as a public holiday.

September 13- *Niños Héroes* Day
This day celebrates the child heroes in Mexico who died defending Chapultepec 1847.

Sep 15 - Independence Day
This day marks independence for El Salvador, Costa Rica, Guatemala, Honduras, and Nicaragua. In Mexico, independence from Spain is celebrated by a communal shout at 11:00 p.m. in remembrance of the first cry of independence. This shout is commonly known as *El Grito* and the holiday itself is known as *Conmemoración de la Proclamación de la Independencia*. In Mexico, this is like an "Independence Day Eve", as Mexican Independence Day is celebrated the following day.

September 16 - Independence Day
Dieciséis de Septiembre is Mexico's Independence Day, not *Cinco de Mayo* as many people believe.

September 18 - Independence Day
This celebrates *Día de la Independencia* for Chile.

September 21 - Independence Day
Belize has celebrated this day as independence from the United Kingdom since 1981.

September 23 - *Grito de Lares*
This is celebrated by Puerto Rico to commemorate the beginning of the movement for independence from Spain.

October

October 12 - Spanish National Day
Día de la Hispanidad is celebrated in Spain, but most other Spanish speaking countries celebrate *Día de la Raza* or Columbus Day. This commemorates the arrival of Columbus in America.

October 10 - *Grito de Yara*
In Cuba, this commemorates the beginning of the revolt against Spain.

October 18 - Our Lord of Miracles
Señor de los Milagros is celebrated in Peru to honor the Purple Christ. Some 300 years ago an earthquake destroyed Lima, leaving a painting of the Purple Christ unharmed.

October 31 to November 2 - Day of the Dead
Day of the Dead or *Día de los Muertos* is a festival celebrated in Mexico and other parts of Central and South America. It is celebrated between October 31st and November 2nd. The celebration of *Día de los Muertos* involves many interesting customs such as the decoration

of sugar skulls and the building of altars to honor one's ancestors.

Day of the Dead Vocabulary
Day of the Dead = *Día de los Muertos*
Flowers= *flores*
Offering= *ofrenda*
Sugar Skulls= *calavera de azúcar*
Yellow Marigold = *cempazuchitl*

Day of the Dead Activities
Gather as much information as you can about Day of the Dead. This holiday is often confused with our celebration of Halloween, so compare and contrast the two holidays with your child. Look up a recipe and cook *Pan de Muerto*. Make and decorate sugar skulls and try any of the other traditions that you wish. Talk to a native about the holiday.

November

November 2 - All Souls' Day
Día de Todos los Santos is celebrated throughout the Catholic Spanish-speaking world to honor the saints.

November 3- Independence Day
Panama celebrates its independence on this day.

November 5 - First Call for Independence
El Salvador Commemorates its first battle for independence on this day.

November 10 - *Fiesta de la Tradición*
Argentina celebrates this festival each year, especially in the town of

San Antonio de Areco.

November 11 - Independence Day
Independence day for Cartagena, Colombia.

November 19 - Feast of Our Lady of Divine Providence
Nuestra Señora de la Divina Providencia is celebrated in Puerto Rico in honor of its patron.

November 20 - Mexican Revolution Day
A Mexican holiday to celebrate the revolution of 1910.

December

December 6 - *Día de la Constitución*
Spain celebrates Constitution Day.

December 8 - Immaculate Conception
Immaculate Conception Day is celebrated in the Catholic world.

December 12 - *Día de la Virgen de Guadalupe*
The Feast Day of our Lady of Guadalupe is celebrated on this day to commemorate the day in 1531 when the Holy Virgin reportedly appeared to Juan Diego. The *Día de la Virgen de Guadalupe* became an national holiday in 1859.

December 16 to 24 -*Las Posadas*
Some Central American countries celebrate *Las Posadas*. This celebration involves visiting family and friends, prayer and song. The holiday has to do with the Virgin's search for a place to stay in Bethlehem. In Colombia, this celebration is called *La Novena*.

Las Posadas Vocabulary

Bethlehem = *Belén*
Family = *Familia*
Jesus = *Jesús*
Joseph = *José*
Mary= *María*
Trip = *Viaje*

Las Posadas Activities

Make a nativity from household items or draw one. You might even make one from cutting out people from magazines and pasting them. Learn some songs in Spanish and sing them. If you have a group of people to participate (such as a language group), set up a route for caroling where people would be willing to open their houses for refreshments.

December 25 – Christmas

In Spanish-speaking countries, Christmas is celebrated differently than in the United States. In some parts of the Spanish-speaking world, shoes are left out instead of stockings. In other parts, gifts are not exchanged on Christmas at all. In Cuba the Christmas holiday was banned in 1969. In Puerto Rico many people pretend to be farmers from the country (*jíbaros*) and wear a straw hat called a *pava* that remains in storage waiting for the Christmas holiday.

Christmas Vocabulary

Angel= *ángel*

Baby= *bebé*

Bethlehem = *Belén*

Christmas= *Navidad*

Gift = *regalo*

Jesus = *Jesús*

Joseph= *José*

Mary= *María*

Shoes= *zapatos*

Song= *canción*

Wise Men = *magos*

Christmas Activities

Look up Christmas traditions for the country of your choice and participate in those that interest you and your child. Take the time to learn some Spanish Christmas songs and sing them often during this season. Don't forget to send holiday greetings to your pen pal if you have one. Look up Christmas recipes from the country of your choice and make as many as possible. Interview a native about his experiences with Christmas.

December 28- *Día de los Inocentes*

This is similar to April Fool's Day and is celebrated in most Spanish-speaking countries. It is a day of tricks and jokes which has its roots in the Catholic commemoration of Herod's order to put all male children to death.

Día de los Inocentes Vocabulary

Joke = *broma*

Laugh = *reír*

Play a prank = *gastar una broma*

Día de los Inocentes Activities

Look up information about the holiday. Play a series of harmless pranks on your child or help your child plan a prank meant for other friends or family members to celebrate this holiday.

December 31 - New Year's Eve

In much of the Spanish-speaking world, the New Year is welcomed at a midnight mass. In Spain, a major celebration takes place near the clock in Madrid in the *Puerta del Sol* much like our New York celebration in Times Square. At the stroke of midnight twelve grapes are gobbled up- one with each chime of the clock.

New Year Vocabulary

Calendar = *calendario*
Clock = *reloj*
Grape = *uva*
Midnight = *medianoche*
New Year = *Año Nuevo*

New Year Activities

Plan a Spanish New Year party with friends or family. Remember that Spain is several hours ahead of the United States, so it will be the New Year there first! If you have Spanish television, watch the *Puerta del Sol* celebration. Make sure each participant has twelve grapes! If you do not have Spanish television, you can just use your own clock.

Pen Pals

Pen Pals as a Cultural Exchange

A pen pal relationship is a unique opportunity to introduce your child to a Spanish speaking culture. These relationships can be an endless source of culturally authentic materials through which to absorb culture. Kids love to send and receive letters and packages. This type of exchange can spark a lifelong interest in the target culture. While it is difficult to find companies that specialize in uniting preschool children, there are many pen pal agencies that can put you in contact with school aged and adult pen pals who might be interested in opening up a family pen pal exchange. Another way to arrange a family pen pal exchange is by talking to native speakers about putting you in contact with a family with children that they know from their home country. Some pen pal agencies can help unite entire classrooms or groups. You might choose to correspond with one pen pal or family or several from the same or different countries.

There are things that you can do to make sure that the pen pal relationship is made as interesting as possible to perpetuate the exchange. Especially for pre-readers, a pen-pal relationship needs to include more than just letters. Make your interaction a full-out cultural exchange.

The exchange of pictures can be very interesting. It is a chance to experience something culturally authentic. Pictures that you will receive from your pen pal are not photographs designed for a textbook or guidebook, but a real glimpse into the life of that culture. You can send your pen pal pictures of your family, of your home and of your city. You should, of course, take proper precautions to ensure safety, especially in the case of a relationship where you might not have reliable references. If your child goes to school, send pictures of the school and of your workplace. Ask your pen pal to do the same.

One way to encourage reciprocation is to mail a disposable camera to your pen pal with instructions about what types of pictures you want and ask him or her to mail the camera back to you when it is full so that you can have it developed. Apart from opening a window into the culture, a photo exchange will open the lines of communication with your pen pal. You will have the opportunity to ask questions about things that you see in the pictures. Keep the dialog open.

The following activities are designed to help you leach as much cultural information as possible out of your pen pal relationship by using the exchange as an ethnographic study (the study of human cultures). As you and your child complete these activities, it will provide both of you with an opportunity to explore your own culture and to compare and contrast it with what you discover about the target culture.

Introductory Culture Capsule

Make an introductory "culture capsule" for your pen pal and ask him or her to do the same. Include cartoons from the Sunday paper, a recipe for a regional dish along with a picture of what it looks like prepared, a schedule outlining a typical day in the life of your family, a favorite candy, a children's book, a fashion magazine and pictures of your child's favorite toys. This will create a springboard for discussion and a more clear idea about what particular cultural aspects you would like to explore.

Sound Tour

Make a recording of your child giving the pen-pal a short message in Spanish. Your child might also include a message in English if your pen pal desires. Give a "sound tour" of your home and city. It is surprising what types of different sounds there are across cultures for things like police and ambulance sirens, telephones and school bells. Some cultures have sounds that do not even exist in this country. For example, Spanish towns often have a man who travels around with a knife sharpener. He blows a whistle to let you know that he is in the area for business. Exchange as many sounds unique to your particular environment as possible.

You might also ask your pen pal to include what sounds animals make in his or her culture (roosters, for instance, say "*qui quiri qui*" and chicks say "*pío*"). Also include the sounds you make to get animals to come to you. My Spanish friends were always amused by how we call a cat in English, as they make a sort of "*pssspssspsss*" sound to attract a cat's attention. You might also compile a collection of 5 to 10 minute segments with recordings in specific locations such as church, the mall, a park, etc. These sound exchanges can be educational to receive and fun to make with your child. When you receive your pen pal's recording, analyze each sound and compare and contrast it with the sounds in your environment.

Home Exchange

Videotape your child giving a tour of your home. First, make sure that your pen pal has the means to watch the video in the format in which you are recording. Keep in mind that you should adjust the amount of information that you give out about yourself and your family depending on how well you know the exchange family. In all likelihood, you will be put in touch with trustworthy people, but be smart about it.

Your child should go through every room in your home and point out any important object. Say the names of different items of furniture and household objects. Describe any item that is particularly meaningful to you and your family and explain why. Focus particularly on any area of the home which you suspect might be different from that of the target country. Additionally, take a tour of your neighborhood and talk about the houses. Ask a close friend or family member if you can also give a tour of their home. If you or your pen pal do not have the means to record a video, then take pictures instead and make notes.

Homes, the things that we keep in them and the way that we make use of space changes drastically from culture to culture. This can be a particularly interesting project. As you analyze your pen pal's home, consider the size of the home, type of furniture used, types of objects in the home, number of possessions and what materials the furniture and homes are made from. Also notice subtle differences, such as they types of doorknobs and locks used on the doors and what the light fixtures and switches look like. Are they similar to the houses that you are familiar with? Are they made of the same materials? Why or why not? Does geography and climate play a role?

Music Exchange

If your pen pal has the means to listen to CDs or tapes, send him or her a compilation of your favorite music along with a list of the most popular music at this time, a current music magazine and anything else related to music in our country. Include information about any kind of regional music that might be interesting such as bluegrass or jazz. If any sort of regional dance is popular in your area, include information on that as well.

Food Exchange

Exchange a food-themed package. Collect and send takeout menus from a variety of local restaurants, pictures of eating establishments, pictures of your family eating at the table, food labels and pictures from each section of your local supermarket. Make a list of foods that are specific to your region, take pictures of the prepared dishes and include recipes. Record what your family eats at each meal for a week and send that to give your pen pal family a more clear idea of what is eaten in your area from day to day.

Exchanging a food package is an interesting way to experience the food culture of another country. You will undoubtedly find some surprising differences in your culture and the target culture. When you receive your food package, experiment with the recipes. Are all of the ingredients readily available at your local supermarket? Does your prepared dish look like the picture that the pen pal sent? What about the supermarket photos? Do the same types of items appear on the shelves? Do you see anything interesting in the produce section that you might ask your pen pal about? Look at the food labels. Is the same type of information available on the food labels in this country as on the food labels from your pen pal? Are any of the brand names the same? Dig a little deeper by looking to see if any of the new brands have websites and visit them. What about the sample restaurant menus? Are the prices comparable to the restaurant prices in this country? What about the hours of operation? In your pen pal's photographs, is the table set the same way that you do it? Examine each item closely.

Time Exchange

Track what each family member does every hour for one week. Take pictures to document some of your activities. With photographs, paper and paste, create a picture story of a day in the life of your child and give information about his or her daily activities under each picture.

When you get your time package from your pen pal, examine it closely. Does your pen pal family seem to wake up at the same time as you or at a different time? How much time is spent for meals? What time does the work day start and stop? Is there a break during the day that we do not have here, such as a siesta? What time does the family go to bed? What types of activities does the family spend the most time on? Additionally, inspect the photographs and see if you notice anything that you have a question about.

Weather and the Environment Exchange

Clip the weather forecast out of a local newspaper for a week or so. If possible, record the forecast from television as well. Take a hike with your family and take pictures of what you see, including animal and plant life. Make sure that the geography of your area is evident in the photographs. See if you can find a list of the median temperatures for your area for each month of the year. You might help your child draw a collection of pictures to depict what he or she perceives the weather to be like during each season.

When you receive your weather package from your pen pal, notice the geography. How might the geography and weather affect daily activities? Do you see a relation between the foods that are eaten in your pen pal's region and what you observe about the climate? Are the seasons the same? How do you think that the weather and climate in your pen pal's area relates to the clothing that you have observed in the photographs that they have sent? Based on what you know, does your pen pal family spend more or less time outdoors than your family? Does geography and climate play a role in this?

Holiday Exchanges

This is a helpful exchange to do in conjunction with some of the holiday activities presented in this section. For each holiday that your family celebrates, take lots of pictures of everything that your family does to send to your pen pal family. Include recipes and photographs of seasonal dishes, recordings of any holiday songs (such as the birthday song or Christmas carols) and an explanation of any special tradition. Include some examples of holiday greeting cards. If your family celebrates the holiday or occasion a different way than most families that you know, explain this. Do this for as many holidays and occasions as possible. Don't forget baptisms, graduations, baby and wedding showers and anything that warrants a parade such as a school homecoming. When you receive a holiday package from your pen pal family, consider whether or not your culture has a similar holiday or celebration. Why do you think that this custom might be different in the target culture? What things are the same? Be sure to ask your pen pal family to explain anything that interests you or makes you curious to know more. Do your own research to see if what your pen pal family is describing lines up with what you have learned from books or the Internet.

School Life Exchange

If your child is in school or preschool, get the teacher's permission to take photographs or video footage documenting the normal day's activities. Send sample projects that your child has worked on in school. Describe our education system, the difference in public and private schools, how many years we go to school here and what we study each year, when you go from a self-contained classroom to changing classes, etc.

When you get your school life package, look at the photographs. Do the classrooms look like the classrooms that you have experience with in your country? How are the students and teachers dressed? Do there appear to be uniforms? Do they go to school at the same times of day and days of the week that we do here?

Style Exchange

Gather some photographs of people you see out at the mall, in church, walking at the trail, on the streets, in schools, in the workplace and wherever else you can. Along with the photographs, send a description of what the clothing styles are currently like for different age groups and for different activities. Along with your photographs, send some current fashion magazines for men and women. In your style package, include information about whether or not things like tattoos are popular and with what age groups, when girls begin wearing makeup and how much they normally wear as well as information on currently popular hairstyles. When you get your style package, closely examine what you find. Are the styles similar or different? How? Why do you think these similarities and differences exist? Do you think that the concept of beauty is the same for your pen pal's culture as it is here? Why or why not?

Toys and Children's Fads Exchange

Every few years, it seems that kids have a new fad. One year it is stick-on earrings, another it is slap bracelets or virtual pets. Record the current fads in your area. Take pictures of the toys, or if they are small, simply send one. Interview several children on what their favorite games, toys, sports and activities are. Clip out ads from magazines and catalogs for popular toys and games.

When you get the report from your pen pal family on popular toys and fads for children, look for similarities and differences in the types of activities which are interesting to children in the target culture. Talk to your child about whether the games and toys that your pen pal family describes would be appealing to him and his or her friends and why or why not.

Manners

Make a list of manners and things that are considered polite and impolite in our society. Think of as many things as possible, ranging from table manners to how to conduct yourself in a school setting. If you can find a way to incorporate photographs, do so. For instance, in some parts of our country, it is impolite to place the elbows on the table while eating. You might take a picture of your child with elbows on the table and the subtitle "impolite" and then a picture of your child with hands folded neatly in lap with the subtitle "polite". This is a good way to explore your own culture as well as learn about another. When you get your manners package from your pen pal, compare and contrast polite and impolite behavior in your culture and in the target culture. Are there things in our culture that are considered polite that are actually impolite in the target culture? Why do you think these things are considered polite or impolite? Does it have anything to do with the values and themes of the target culture? Explore these ideas.

Gestures and Body Language

The meaning of gestures and body language can change drastically from culture to culture and it is well worth investigating the differences before traveling abroad. I'll never forget the time that I was the only American on a team of British instructors teaching English in Spain. I was passing out worksheets and came up short. The guy from London standing next to the stack of papers asked me how many I needed. I flashed two fingers. "Two!" Jaws dropped. The Brits stared at me in disbelief. "What? I need two." I continued to wave the two fingers in the air. Everyone was frozen, horrified. Wide-eyed, he handed me my two worksheets and I continued teaching Spaniards about clothing vocabulary. I later discovered that I had inadvertently offended my fellow teachers by flashing an unsavory hand gesture.

This is a common scenario among foreigners visiting another country. It is easy to give people the wrong idea just by using body language that might come quite naturally to you. This is especially true of people from low context cultures (such as Germany or the United States) visiting high context cultures (such as Spain or China). In a low context culture such as ours, we generally say what we mean. Our body language is secondary to what comes out of our mouths. In high context cultures, much of what is said is nonverbal. Learning the nonverbal language of a culture can be as important as learning the spoken language. The following activities are ways for you to get to know a little about the nonverbal communication of your target culture.

Movies

Get some movies or television shows that were made in the target culture. Pay special attention to the gestures and body language used in certain situations- especially gestures that you do not see often in our culture. Make a note of these gestures and continue to watch. Each time you see the same gesture, make a note of the situation in which it was presented. See if you can make a connection between the situation and the gesture. Practice the gestures that you have learned by using a role play with your child.

Native Speaker Practice

Next time you are practicing your Spanish with a native speaker, pay special attention to his or her body language and gestures. Does the native speaker move his or her body in the same way as people in this country? If you were watching this person speak from across the room, would you know that he or she was not speaking English just by watching the gestures? What differences are there in the nonverbal communication of his or her culture? Ask the native speaker specifically about what gestures he or she has noticed in our country and ask for help in learning about the nonverbal communication of the target culture.

Internet Search

From time to time, there are studies that appear about the nonverbal communication of certain cultures. Do an Internet search for studies that are specific to the culture that you are learning about. Practice the new gestures that you learn with your child in a role play.

Gesture Study

Some of the educational suppliers listed in the resource directory (such as Teacher's Discovery) routinely carry charts and books on gestures and body language from different cultures. Consider obtaining some of this material and make a formal study of the gestures and body language of the target culture. Whatever you learn, practice it in your Spanish conversation group and get feedback from natives about your use of the gestures. Teach the gestures to your child by using them in the correct situation as you speak Spanish. In this way, the nonverbal communication of the target culture will be linked to language learning and will be produced naturally by the child as he or she communicates in the target culture.

Interviewing Native Speakers

Interviewing native speakers is a great way to learn about the culture of another country. Most people will be glad to help you learn about their home culture if you simply ask. You can talk to the native speakers in your conversation group or intercambio program or you can find native speakers on the Internet for a voice chat. Be mindful, of course, of the inherent dangers of Internet communication and take the proper precautions.

Below you will find some suggested questions to ask native speakers about specific topics to help guide you in exploring the new culture. Have your child help you conduct the interview or simply conduct the interview yourself and then incorporate what you have learned into your child's language activities.

Food

1.What types of foods are most common in your region?
2.What is your favorite food?
3.Do you find anything strange about the food we eat in this country?
4.How is our food different from yours?
5.Is eating in a restaurant a different experience in your country than it is here? Why or why not?
6.What are supermarkets like in your country?
7.Does your family eat together often?
8.What time of day are your mealtimes?
9.What are typical breakfast, lunch and dinner foods?

Love

1. What are dating rituals like in your country?
2. How do couples normally meet one another?

3. How long do people typically court before marriage?

4. What is the typical age for someone to marry in your country?

5. What are weddings like? Are they different from those in our country?

6. Are there special foods eaten at weddings? Special music?

7. What do people wear to weddings in your country?

8. What do people give as wedding gifts in your country?

Friendship

1. How do most friends know one another in your country. Do they meet through family, work, hobbies, etc.?

2. Is it typical to have one close-knit group of friends or to participate in social activities with a variety of casual acquaintances?

3. Do you think that the way we interact with our friends is the same or different in this country?

4. What are activities that you normally do with your friends?

5. Do friends normally talk on the telephone with one another as much as they do here?

6. On what occasions do friends exchange gifts? What types of gifts are exchanged?

7. Does a friend typically wait for an invitation to visit another friend's house, or is it acceptable just to drop in unannounced?

Home and Family Life

1. How many family members normally live in a house?

2. How are houses different or the same in your country? Are they the same size? What materials are they made of? What else is different or the same?

3. How long do children normally live in the home before moving out?

4. How many children are in the typical family?

5. How are children normally disciplined in your country? Do you

think that children's rules of behavior are the same or different here and in your country?

6. Do children normally feel comfortable talking to their parents or other family members about problems?

7. Is the extended family a close-knit group?

8. From what you have observed, what do you think is different or the same regarding how we relate to our families in this country and in your country?

General Questions

1. Has any difference that you have seen in this country particularly surprised you?

2. How are our schools and workplaces different or the same?

3. Do any of our customs or manners seem strange to you? What are they like in your country?

4. Do people in our country do the same things for fun as they do in your country?

5. Do people wear the same types of clothing in your country as they do here? What is the same and what is different?

Part IV
As They Grow

Continuing Spanish Through the Years

Childhood

Once you have completed the thematic vocabulary exercises in this book with your child, you will undoubtedly want to keep the momentum alive by creating your own activities with vocabulary sets that you have selected yourself. Use the following guidelines to create your own activities:

1. Choose a vocabulary set to work with that will be useful in your child's life. For instance, if your family owns a dry cleaning business, you might have a dry cleaning theme. Build a vocabulary list consisting of words and expressions that one needs in order to function in that environment. You might include words such as "iron," "washer," "press," "fold," "cash register," "ticket" and "detergent." Look up the words in a dictionary and, if possible, ask a native speaker to look over your list to make sure that the words that you have are the ones that are really used in the target country. A great place to ask advice on vocabulary and expressions is in the online forums at WordReference. com. More information about WordReference is given in the resource directory under the subject of online dictionaries.

2. Once you have compiled all of your vocabulary and have learned it yourself, begin to incorporate it into your normal conversations with your child. Be a little creative. If conversations about dry cleaning do not just come up naturally, take your child on a tour of the family business. Let your child hear the vocabulary enough times that the language is internalized. Avoid sitting your child down to memorize a list of vocabulary out of its normal context. Vocabulary should always be presented in context- not in isolation in the form of a vocabulary list.

3. Once you have presented the vocabulary to your child and your child has become familiar with it, orchestrate situations in which your child must practice the vocabulary. These situations can be practical,

such as a Spanish-only day helping you with the family business or in the form of games and activities. Remember that vocabulary games such as bingo, rayuela, card games like cucaracha, charades and pictionary can be modified to fit any vocabulary set. So can many projects such as picture dictionaries.

4. Once your child has learned and practiced the vocabulary, don't let it die! Continue to recycle the vocabulary in future activities to maintain it.

School Age Children

School age children become quite busy with homework and extracurricular activities such as sports and don't have time for quite as many lengthy activities with mom or dad. Fortunately, your language ability as well as your child's will have grown by this time and you will simply be able to converse in Spanish whenever you are together to maintain and grow in the language. Continue to provide your child with quality materials such as books, movies and games in Spanish. Also keep up your participation in your bilingual community activities or intercambio program. By this time, Spanish will be a normal part of your family life.

Your child's school may offer an elementary Spanish program that he or she can participate in. If this is the case, your child will probably begin to learn about Spanish grammar just like he or she will learn about English grammar. Maybe there will be other Spanish speaking children to talk to. Continue to encourage your child's use of and exposure to the language in a variety of settings throughout the early school years.

Preteens and Teens

Your child as a preteen or teen will have an advantage over those who are just beginning the language learning process. He or she has had the opportunity to learn and practice the language before the intense insecurity of the adolescent years has had a chance to kick in.

When teenagers show up in a high school Spanish class, they are reluctant to try and say foreign words and terrified of looking silly in front of their peers. Even if they are interested in language learning, they are often unlikely to express the interest because it is not considered "cool." Their self-consciousness hinders their language learning ability. Teenagers who already have some speaking ability in the language in a high school Spanish class might pretend not to know as much for fear of being seen as a show-off. Either way, a high school language class is not likely to be a comfortable place for a teenager.

Don't rely on your child's high school language program to continue to grow your child's Spanish fluency. It will be up to you to provide interesting opportunities for your preteen or teenage child to continue with his or her Spanish practice. Continue to provide interesting and quality resources for your child in the form of books, movies, music and magazines. Consider planning family trips to Spanish-speaking locations or allowing him or her to participate in volunteer programs abroad with a church or service organization. Continue to make speaking Spanish a normal part of your family life and take part in plenty of activities with your bilingual community. Allowing your child to take college classes as part of an Early Scholar or Dual Enrollment program can help to boost your child's confidence as well as provide a way to get ahead academically. Consider an exchange or study abroad program for your child if he or she is interested.

High school is a good time to encourage your child to begin a third language, since he or she will probably have a choice of languages to study. Having already been exposed to a second language, your child will probably find it very easy to learn a third. This can boost confidence and make the school experience more enjoyable overall.

Part V
Resources

Evaluating Resources and Materials

As long as you are the facilitator for your child's journey into the language and culture of another country, it will be up to you to choose quality resources and materials for that journey. The following is a list of some of the most basic resources and materials that you will probably be using and criteria to consider when selecting them.

Books

Like almost all other materials, the first thing that you should look for in a book is cultural authenticity. Your child will be learning culture as well as language when he or she is reading. Otherwise, make sure the book is about a topic that will be interesting to your child. Don't bore your child to tears with something that they would not like in English just because you happened to find it in Spanish. Use the sites listed in the resource directory to choose something that your child will like. Also, make sure that the books are on his or her level intellectually, not just linguistically. Many children will be put off by a book that seems too babyish or too complicated with too few pictures, regardless of whether or not they can understand the text. Illustrations should be interesting and high quality and the type should be easy to read.

Dictionaries

A good dictionary is indispensable in a language learning endeavor. The best Spanish-English dictionaries will give you clues as to which words are most prevalent in which countries as well as giving you sample sentences so that you can see the usage in context. These features will serve to disambiguate words that can have more than one meaning and help to give you an idea of the connotation that the word carries. There are several online dictionaries mentioned in the resource directory that serve these functions.

One trick to making sure that the dictionary is giving you the word that you are looking for is this: when you look up a word in the English-Spanish section, take the Spanish word and look it up in the Spanish-English section. Sometimes this gives you a completely different word. If this is the case, pick another English word that is a synonym for the word that you want and look it up in the same way until you get the word that you want.

Magazines

Many of the activities presented in this book, if you do not like to draw, include the use of magazines. The best magazine pictures to use are those that are culturally authentic. The reason for this is that the images that appear will be from the culture that you are learning about, which will allow your child to absorb the language and culture simultaneously. For instance, if your target culture is that of Spain and you and your child are working on a food-themed project, it would be better if your child learned the word *leche* alongside a picture of boxed milk than a picture of a plastic jug because then the word is associated with the correct mental image of the product. Additionally, authentic magazines are bound to contain a plethora of interesting items aside from just the images that you can use, such as recipes.

Aside from cultural authenticity, try to find a magazine that will give you the most bang for your buck, visually speaking. If you have only women's beauty magazines to work from when you are creating a picture bank for an activity about animals, you are likely to come up short. Try to collect magazines that offer images over a wide range of topics and that include engaging, interesting pictures that you are likely to be able to use for a variety of different activities.

Movies

It is wonderful if you can find age-appropriate, culturally authentic movies for your child. In this way, your child can absorb many cultural details that are often simply not present in print material, such as the use of body language. However, the United States is universally known for its high quality, high budget, high-in-special-effects movies. Resultantly, children from our country who are used to watching these movies on a regular basis normally have very high standards when it comes to cinematography. Movies from other countries rarely make the grade for them. Kids who have not been exposed to much television sometimes escape this cinematic snobbery, but for those who remain picky, it is best to just bite the bullet and let them watch old favorites with Spanish audio, even if the words don't match the mouths.

Native Speakers

Ok, so native speakers are not really a material, but they are a type of resource and there are things you have to consider before choosing one to formally work on your language with. Consider the fact that educated individuals are easier to understand than those who are not quite as educated.

Remember way back in the frequently asked questions when we talked about the different dialects and we discussed the fact that there is sort of a "standard" Spanish as well as English? This standard language is low in colloquialisms and is almost universally understood (the language used for news reports and the like). Well, educated speakers are more likely to use language closer to that standard than uneducated people. Think about how a college English professor might invite you to dinner versus dear old Aunt Dotty who dropped out of school in the sixth grade. Professor Jones might say, "Good evening. Would you like to join me for dinner?" Aunt Dotty might say, "Hidey Doo. I ain't had nutin' to eat all day. Yonna come eat supper?" While Aunt Dotty might make a far more entertaining and enjoyable dinner date than Professor Smith, she is going to be infinitely more difficult to understand.

Educated people also seem to naturally modify their language when speaking to a foreigner, cutting out confusing idioms and clearly enunciating the words. Uneducated people, for whatever reason, don't normally do this. When speaking to a foreign person, these individuals simply seem to get louder, which doesn't help much. Of course, I'm generalizing here. Everyone is different.

I'm not saying that you need to steer clear of uneducated people and only associate with people who are educated. Sometimes the people who lack formal education are the most wise, giving us profound insight into the underlying values of a culture as well as being the most interesting. However, putting yourself in a situation with a native speaker that you can not understand early on in the language learning process can undermine your confidence in your language ability and make you reluctant to practice speaking as much as you should.

General Evaluation Criteria

In general, when you are evaluating a material, ask yourself these questions:

1. Is it culturally authentic?
2. Is it at the right level linguistically and intellectually for the child?
3. Is it interesting?
4. Would my child enjoy this item if it were in English?
5. Does it provide comprehensible input?

Resource Directory

Adult Language Programs

Rosetta Stone

Website: http://www.rosettastone.com

Address: Rosetta Stone135 W Market StHarrisonburg, VA 22801

In my opinion, Rosetta Stone is one of the best language software programs available for adults. It is a relatively expensive program, but certainly worth it if you are committed to learning another language on your own. You learn quickly and easily with this program and you are spared boring grammar lessons. The lessons are engaging and effective and your child might enjoy doing the lessons with you.

Pimsleur Spanish

Websites: http://www.pimleurdirect.com

http://www.pimleuraudio.com

http://www.pimleurapproach.com

The Pimsleur Language Series uses the Audiolingual Method (ALM) to teach a foreign language. Pimsleur focuses on language that you will use in a travel situation. In my opinion, ALM is not the optimal way to learn a language, but this program does have the advantage of concise 30 minute lessons that you can do in your car. There is no need to take time out to sit down with a notebook or at the computer to complete these lessons. Lessons are conducted by native speakers and are excellent for practicing pronunciation. I completed the first 10 lessons of Pimsleur French before going to France, and I learned enough to get by. I recommend this system to adults who have a long commute and little extra time to learn a language. This program is available from the websites listed above and most major bookstores

Au Pair Programs

There are many Au Pair agencies out there. The best way to choose an agency is to gather information from as many as possible and then to choose the one that best fits your needs. Information and regulations regarding the Au Pair program for foreign nationals between 18 and 26 years of age from the U.S. Department of State can be found at: http://exchanges.state.gov/education/jexchanges/private/aupair. htm

Culture Care Au Pair
Website: http://www.culturalcare.com
Address: One Education Street, Cambridge, MA 02141

EurAupair
Website: http://www.euraupair.com
Address: EurAupair Eastern Office, 407 N. Washington St. #1, Alexandria, VA 22314
See website for other office addresses.

Interexchange
Website: http://www.aupairusa.org
Address: Au Pair USA161 Sixth Avenue New York, NY 1001

Author Online

LinguaCulture
Website: http://www.linguaculture.net

This is my own website. Check for updates, printable resources, lesson plans and other fun stuff!

Children's Books

Amazon

Website: http://www.amazon.com

Amazon offers new and used books both in Spanish and about Spanish-speaking countries and culture. You can even search Listmania, which will give you lists of books, DVDs, CDs and other products that Amazon users recommend. Another nice feature on Amazon is that it provides customer ratings and comments for the products.

Barahona Center

Website: http://www.csusm.edu/csb
Address: California State University San Marcos ,Kellogg Library, 5th Floor333 S Twin Oaks Valley Road, San Marcos, California 92096-0001

Barahona Center for the Study of Books in Spanish for Children and Adolescents has an excellent searchable database that allows you to look for Spanish children's books by age, subject, grade level, publisher, subject and even country. When you click on a book, you can find out everything about it, including where it has been reviewed. This site is particularly useful for finding books to reinforce vocabulary for a specific theme that you are working on.

Shen's Books

Website: http://www.shens.com
Address: 1547 Palos Verdes Mall #291 Walnut Creek, CA 94597

Shen's Books offers multicultural literature for children both in English and in other languages, many of them authentic. They do offer a limited catalog, but the full selection of books is only available on the website.

The Reading Tub
Website: http://www.thereadingtub.com

The Reading Tub has a list of Foreign Language books for children that have been reviewed by both a younger and an older child. The Reading Tub gives pros and cons for each book and gives an opinion on whether you should borrow the book, buy the book or skip it altogether.

Children's Educational Resources

Enchanted Learning
Website: http://www.enchantedlearning.com

Enchanted Learning has both free resources and resources for paid members. It has hundreds of printable coloring books, crafts, picture dictionaries and labeling worksheets in Spanish.

Language Lizard
Website: http://www.languagelizard.com

Language Lizard offers a variety of multilingual and multicultural products of interest to parents of young children.

Mundo Latino
Website: http://www.mundolatino.org

Mundo Latino offers a variety of useful links to almost anything imaginable in Spanish: online illustrated children's stories with audio, games, coloring books, articles about celebrities, etc. There is also a parent and teacher section.

Teacher's Discovery
Website: http://teachersdiscovery.com
Address: Teacher's Discovery - Foreign Language 2741 PaldanDrive, Auburn Hills, Mi 48326

Teacher's Discovery has an extensive range of educational products including games, toys, culturally authentic fake foods, craft kits, books, posters, stickers and seasonal items. They have an excellent catalog.

Children's Language Programs and Classes

Flip Flop Spanish by Suzanne Gose
Website: http://www.flipflopspanish.com

Futura Language Professionals (Director: Kara O'Reilly)
Website: http://wwwfuturaadventures.com

Magic Spanish for Kids
Website: http://www.bethmanners.com

Muzzy Language Program
Website: http://www.early-advantage.com

Spanish for Preschoolers by Ana Lomba
Website: http://www.spanishforpreschoolers.com

Spanish Workshop for Children by Marcela Summerville
Website: http://www.spanishworkshopforchildren.com

Country and Culture Information Online

Country Reports
Website : http://www.countryreports.org

Country Reports is not a free website, but it is an excellent resource. You can go to the website for information about a free sample country to see what you can get. For each country, you can see accurate cultural information including recipes, fashion, language, home and family life, social customs and gestures, history, maps, photo galleries, national symbols, current events and play learning games about the country.

World Factbook
Website: https://www.cia.gov/library/publications/the-world-factbook

This website by the CIA offers up-to-date facts about every country in the world. This is a nice, free quick reference for finding a country profile.

Embassies
If you plan to travel, writing the embassy is an can help you to learn about entry requirements, secure necessary paperwork, get current travel warnings and much more. Even if you don't plan to travel, writing an embassy can provide you with useful information for a project. Writing an embassy also gives your child valuable practice with letter writing, a skill that often goes unused in today's web-based world.

European Embassies

Spain
2375 Pennsylvania Avenue, NW, Washington DC 20037

Central American Embassies

Belize
2535 Massachusetts Ave. NW, Washington DC 20008

Guatemala
2220 R Street, NW, Washington DC 20008

Honduras
3007 Tilden Street, NW, Suite 4M, Washington DC 20008

El Salvador
2308 California Street, NW, Washington DC20008

The Republic of Nicaragua
1627 New Hampshire Avenue, NW, Washington DC 20009

Costa Rica
2114 S Street, NW, Washington DC 20008

The Republic of Panama
2862 McGill Terrace, NW, Washington DC 20008

Caribbean Embassies

Cuba Interests Section
2630 and 2639 16th Street, NW, Washington DC 20009

The Dominican Republic
1715 22nd Street, NW, Washington DC 20008

North American Embassies

Mexico
1911 Pennsylvania Avenue, NW, Washington DC 20006

South American Embassies

The Republic of Venezuela
1099 30th Street NW, Washington DC 20007

Colombia
2118 Leroy Place, NW, Washington DC 20008

Ecuador
2535 15th Street, NW, Washington DC 20009

Peru
1700 Massachusetts Avenue, NW, Washington DC 20036

Bolivia
3014 Massachusetts Avenue, NW, Washington DC 20008

Paraguay
2400 Massachusetts Avenue, NW, Washington DC 20008

Chile
1732 Massachusetts Avenue, NW, Washington DC 20036

Argentina

1600 New Hampshire Avenue, NW, Washington DC 20009

Uruguay

1913 I (Eye) Street, NW, Washington DC 20006

African Embassies

Equatorial Guinea

2020 16th Street, NW, Washington DC 20009

Exchange Programs

Academic Foundation for International Cultural Exchange

Website: http://www.afice.org

Address: Academic Foundation for International Cultural Exchange7242 La Jolla BoulevardLa Jolla, CA 92037

American Institute for Foreign Study

Website: http://www.aifs.com

Address: American Institute For Foreign StudyRiver Plaza, 9 West BroadStreetStamford, CT 06902

Center for Cultural Interchange

Website: http://www.cci-exchange.com

Address: Center for Cultural InterchangeNational Office746 North LaSalle DriveChicago, IL 60610

Foundation for Intercultural Travel

Website: http://www.fitamerica.org

Address: Foundation for Intercultural Travel P.O. Box 3102Matthews, NC 28106-3102

Student Exchange Alliance

Website: http://www.sea-usa.org

Address: Student Exchange Alliance421 E Jefferson St.Tipton, IN 46072

Free Online Dictionaries and Translation Sites

Spanishdict

Website: http://www.spanishdict.com

Spanishdict is a basic, free online dictionary with audiosupport.

Freetranslation

Website: http://www.freetranslation.com

Freetranslation lets you copy and paste foreign text into an automatic translator. You can go from English to Spanish (or other languages) or Spanish to English. Be warned: the translation software can be somewhat useful for figuring out the gist of a text, but do not trust it for an accurate translation. To see what I mean, try typing in something familiar like the American Pledge of Allegiance. Copy the Spanish translation that it gives you and have the software put it back into English again. It should say the exact same thing that you started with, right? Nope! You'll get some strange stuff. Translation software is not the same as having a person translate something. Translation software generally translates word-for-word, which is not accurate, so don't use it for something like translating an English letter to a pen pal into Spanish.

Wordreference

Website: http://www.wordreference.com

Wordreference.com offers a free dictionary that goes from Spanish to English or English to Spanish (and many other languages as well). You can click on a word to hear how it is pronounced. This site includes a very useful Spanish thesaurus as well as a verb conjugator and also connects to language forums where you can get feedback from native speakers on slang and colloquial language that generally does not appear in a standard dictionary. This is one of my personal favorite online dictionary sites.

Language Camps

Concordia

Website: http://www.clvweb.cord.edu/prweb
Address: Concordia Language Villages901 8th St S., Moorhead, MN 56562

Concordia offers a wide range of immersion language experiences ranging from one weekend to several weeks for individuals or families. There is often a waiting list for these programs, so make plans well in advance.

Language Conservatory

Website: http://www.languageconservatory.com
Address: The Language Conservatory, LLC14151 Montfort Dr., Suite 216 Dallas, Texas 75254

Language Conservatory offers camps for students K-12 in Texas. Early registration is recommended for these camps. Family instruction and customized programs are also available.

The Children's Arts Corner

Website: http://www.artscorner.com

Address:1403 Massachusetts AvenueLexington MA 02420

The Children's Arts Corner has ongoing programs and a summer camp program for preschoolers through grade schoolers that includes art and ballet.

Online Communities

Online communities are an easy way to make contact with other language learners and families raising bilingual children. You can share experiences and ask advice from other parents or organize a resource exchange.

Bicultural Family

Website: http://www.biculturalfamily.org

Bicultural Family offers discussion forums, articles and other useful information including a listing of bilingual playgroups. It is also the home of an excellent online magazine called *Multilingual Living*.

Bilingual Families Connect

Website: http://www.bilingualfamiliesconnect.com

This website allows you to connect and communicate with families with similar interests. There are a variety of resources available including articles, discussion forums and helpful tips.

Google
Website: http://www.groups.google.com

Similar to yahoo groups, you can start a local group or keep the group strictly online.

Livejournal
Website: http://www.livejournal.com

Livejournal has thousands of online communities for an information exchange on different topics. You can create a free account or upgrade to a paid account for more options. You can search communities by interest or search for other Livejournal users in your area with similar interests. You can also start your own community for free.

Meetup
Website: http://www.meetup.com

There are thousands of Meetup groups for various topics. You can search your city to see if someone has already started a Spanish conversation group, materials exchange, bilingual playgroup or other language group in your area. You can organize your own group for a fee.

Tribe
Website: http://www.tribe.com

Tribe is similar to Meetup - you can search your local area to see if someone has already begun a Spanish group or you can start your own.

Yahoo

Website: http://www.groups.yahoo.com

With yahoo groups, you can start a local group or you can keep the group strictly online.

Online Language Learning Programs and Resources

Spanicity

Website: http://www.spanicity.com

Spanicity offers many free Spanish lessons with audio support, including the Spanish alphabet.

StudySpanish

Website: http://www.studyspanish.com

StudySpanish offers Spanish lessons with audio support for free, however there are some features that come only with a paid account. Many of my students and friends have reported some success with these lessons.

123Teachme

Website: http://www.123teachme.com

123teachme has free thematically organized Spanish lessons and downloadable videos to aid learning.

Online Travel Resources

Let's Go

Website: http://www.letsgo.com

The Let's Go site is an great travel resource with suggested itineraries, tips for traveling on a budget and maps along with interesting tidbits about each destination. Each year, Let's Go puts out updated travel guides that are widely available in bookstores. These guides are written by young authors who are forced to travel on a shoestring budget, seeking out the best accommodation for the money and writing honest reviews of everything they find. They include everything you need: train and bus schedules, a list of restaurants and how much you should expect to pay at each, must-see attractions along with prices and times of operation, areas of town to avoid, which hostals have friendly owners and so forth. In my opinion, this is the most useful travel guide out there and it is certainly worth the extra bulk in your backpack.

Fodor's

Website: http://www.fodors.com

The Fodor's website is full of useful information about travel destinations, including cultural information and suggested itineraries. Like Let's Go, Fodor's offers updated printed travel guides each year for sale in bookstores. Fodor's makes excellent travel guides, but these guides are geared more towards tourists than the free-spirited traveler.

Frommers

Website: http://www.frommers.com

The Frommers website is probably the most comprehensive online travel guide. You can look up what interests you about each destination by category (beaches, vineyards, castles, cathedrals, etc.). It gives you information and telephone numbers for each location. This site gives you history, cultural information, guides to art and architecture, tips for special-needs travelers, information on health insurance abroad and much more. Frommers also offers a print travel guide for many locations updated each year.

U.S. Department of State

Website: http://www.travel.state.gov

This government website publishes current travel warnings, security guidelines and information on passports and visas.

Pen Pal Exchanges

A Girl's World

Website: http://www.agirlsworld.com
Address: A Girl's World Online Clubhouse, P.O. Box 153551, San Diego, CA 92195-3551

Epals

Website: http://www.epals.com

This is the best resource that I have seen for connecting learners from around the globe.

Student Letter Exchange

Website: http://www.pen-pal.com

Address: Student Letter Exchange, 211 Broadway, Suite 201Lynbrook, NY 11563

World Pen Pals

Website: http://www.world-pen-pals.com/

Address: World Pen Pals, P.O. Box 337Saugerties, NY12477

List of Spanish Speaking Countries

Europe

Spain

Carribean

Cuba
Dominican Republic
Puerto Rico

Central America

Belize (although the official language is English)
Costa Rica
El Salvador
Guatemala
Honduras
Nicaragua
Panamá

North America

United States (especially the Southwest)

South America

Venezuela
Colombia
Ecuador
Peru
Bolivia
Paraguay
Chile
Argentina
Uruguay

Africa

Equatorial Guinea

Linguistic and Education Terms

Acculturation: adopting the social patterns of another culture

Audiolingual Method: method of language learning based on repetitive drills and memorization of set phrases

Cognate: a word that looks or sounds the same in two different languages

Comprehensible Input: language that one can understand

Critical Period: an age range during which a human's brain is optimally hardwired to acquire language

Culturally Authentic Materials: materials that are meant for people in the culture in which it was produced, not for foreign learners

Enculturation: learning the social patterns of your own culture

Ethnography: the study of human cultures

Heritage Speaker: a speaker who is not a native speaker of a language nor a foreign language learner, but who has learned a language through natural means away from the country of origin, perhaps from a parent

High Context Culture: a culture which carries a high level of complex nonverbal communication

Idiom: expression which carries a different meaning than what it literally says. For example, "it's raining cats and dogs" does not literally mean that cats and dogs are falling from the sky, but that it is raining hard

Implicit Language System: the language that is readily accessible for a speaker to call upon when participating in live conversation

Instantiation: choosing which schema to apply to a certain situation

Language Acquisition: language learning that happens not through direct instruction but indirectly through exposure to the language

Language Internalization: depositing language into the implicit language system

Low Context Culture: a culture which carries a low level of complex nonverbal communication

Meaningful drills: language drills in which the learner must attend to the meaning of the language and which can not be completed mechanically

Monochronic Time: the treatment of time as a rigid structure

Native Speaker: one who has acquired a language within its country of origin as his or her primary language

Phonemic Awareness: awareness of sound patterns within a language

Polychronic Time: treatment of time as a flexible, fluid entity

Schema: background knowledge of a certain subject or situation

Target Country: the country that one wishes to learn about

Target Culture: the culture that one wishes to learn about

Target Language: the language that one wishes to learn about

About the Author

Starr Weems de Graffenried has been a Spanish and art teacher in the Limestone County school system for six years . She is a college Dual Enrollment teacher, a private Spanish instructor for children and she has designed the curriculum for foreign language workshops. She holds a M.Ed. In Foreign Language Curriculum and Teaching from Auburn University and is CELTA certified through Cambridge for teaching English as a second language to Adults. She has studied abroad in Spain and Germany. She is a certified Yoga instructor and she enjoys playing with her two children, learning languages, reading, teaching and spending time with her husband. Visit her website at www.linguaculture.net.

Printed in the United States
95664LV00004B/27/A